Recycle and Grow Rich!

How to set up a profitable and scalable e-waste recycling business

D.B. Prabhu

(Founder and CEO of Respose Waste Management and Research Pvt Ltd)

ISBN   9781648505669

Acknowledgements

At the outset let me admit that this book is a result of the collective effort of many people. I was perhaps just instrumental in putting it all together in a book form. Sincere thanks to all the great business people, environmental activists, public policy students, researchers and fellow authors who shared with me their insights and passions. It is impossible to name all of them and lest I make the mistake of being judgmental about anyone, let me simply express my gratitude to one and all. All of their advice went a long way in putting together these many varied ideas in a practical way.

I sincerely thank all my business colleagues for their valuable suggestions and for taking on my workload and allowing me to have my space during the long hours of writing even during office time. I am also thankful to all my family members – my mother, father, wife and son for bearing with me while I put in the time and effort into the creation of this book.

Special thanks to Rucha Kochrekar for designing and great cover page. Rucha went out of the way to bring on design after design until it satisfied me. And she did all of it with a great smile.

Lastly, this may be just right an opportunity to thank my publishers M/S Notion Press Inc. and Notion Press Media Pvt Ltd for taking the efforts to publish my work.

Author's Note

e-waste recycling is getting a lot of glamour by virtue of the press. Almost every week I see some articles talking about e-waste and more often than not they talk about two aspects – (a) the pollution caused by e-waste mishandling and (b) the gold and other precious metals content in e-waste. The second part invariably attracts the entrepreneurial mind. Such entrepreneurs, both existing or aspiring then start looking up a lot of literature on the internet which only helps in overwhelming them even more.

Having been instrumental in setting up more than 20 e-waste recycling facilities for my customers, and having consulted many more, I have a reasonable insight into the business and am equipped with the correct and relevant knowledge. This book will help the readers to eliminate the clutter from the data available in the public domain and absorb only important and useful information.

The objective of writing this book is to help fellow entrepreneurs understand the nuances of setting up an e-waste recycling business. After reading this book, the reader will be able to understand the e-waste market, existing e-waste handling practices, International regulations, India specific regulations, the e-waste business model and its variations, risks and risk mitigation methods. Apart from the core domain knowledge of e-waste recycling, he/she will also be able to get a detailed insight into the actual setting up of the business and ideas to run it successfully.

Disclaimer

This book is based on information available to the author through various sources. The author has verified the authenticity of the information within the limits of his bounded rationality and thus the overall representation may suffer from agency effects.

The views and opinions expressed in this article are those of the author and do not necessarily reflect any official policy or position. All analyses performed within this article are within the bounded rationality of the author and based on the limited and dated resources available to him. Although every effort has been made to ensure that the information herein is correct the author does not assume ownership of the same and hereby disclaims any liability to any party for any loss, damage, disruption, disrepute or any other consequences caused by errors or omissions, whether such errors or omissions result from negligence, accident, or any other cause. Hence all information contained herein should be utilized for any purposes only after due diligence from the applicable relevant perspective.

Introduction

Congratulations on your decision to pick up this book. You are about to unlock the secrets to making tons of money from e-waste recycling. However, to be able to do that you need to promise certain things to yourself. So put your hand on your heart and say it aloud,

> "I am not looking at a get rich quick scheme. I am willing to invest my efforts, time and money into building a long-lasting profitable and scalable business."

Now that you have taken this oath solemnly, let me also promise you certain things. At the end of this book,

- I will empower you with the domain knowledge related to e-waste business.
- I will show you the tricks for structuring a profitable business
- I will help you with a blueprint template for your business plan

Having made these promises to each other, let me also explain to you how this book is laid out.

The book starts with some basics of business, entrepreneurial characteristics and the demands of the waste management sector. The 1st chapter highlights general but key entrepreneurial values needed to succeed in the waste management sector.

In the next chapter, we look at an overview of e-waste in general and take into consideration certain qualitative facts about the e-waste market. This chapter should show you the good and not so good sides of the business.

The 3rd chapter is about current practices in the e-waste space and can help you to give you an idea about various areas where you can add value.

The 4th chapter is about comprehensive market analysis and it should help to let you decide your own positioning within the market space from the point of view of your strengths and available opportunities.

Collection is usually the bone of contention for most aspiring entrepreneurs exploring the e-waste space. The 5th chapter gives many ideas for collection and fires your skills of imagination to expand further on the same.

The 6th chapter explains various business models that one can explore in the e-waste space.

The next chapter explains shopfloor processes and technologies for various functions in e-waste recycling.

Chapter 8 is about technology evaluation and tips for selecting your technology providers.

Financial viability and calculation methods are discussed in Chapter 9 with some examples and some sample numbers.

Chapter 10 talks about the risks of getting in the e-waste business and ways to mitigate those risks.

Chapter 11 is about regulations and compliances required and desirable for the e-waste management business.

Finally, in Chapter 12, we look at a template for creating an effective business plan document and creating a blueprint for setting up your business.

At the end of each of the chapters, there is a small exercise for you to do. You may decide to sit with a wad of papers and a pen or a pencil. As you reach the end of the book you are likely to have a great business plan ready.

While this book is written from the perspective of e-waste, the methods applied and the thought process developed can be applied to any other business, especially if it has anything to do with recycling.

Enjoy creating your new world!

Chapter 1

e-Waste recycling – the big why

Any business is driven on the fuel of the entrepreneur's passion. Of course, there are many supporting elements, individuals and environmental conditions on which business thrives. But in adverse or challenging conditions the singular element that keeps businesses kicking is the mettle of the entrepreneur.

So, if you are even remotely thinking of getting into a business, the first thing that you must do is to be clear about why you want to do it in the first place. Questions such as which business to get in and how to set it up come much later.

If you are a fresh entrepreneur, you need to ask yourself your reasons for getting into a business. If you feel that your reasons are anything like plenty of freedom, no accountability, lots of money, and other esoteric stuff, please be warned that it is nothing like that. Setting up any new business demands a huge amount of time, effort and money. You are accountable for practically everything and you may as well say goodbye to weekends and holidays for the first couple of years. The clock will cease to exist for you and you may have several instances of being broke, cold and hungry. If you have the stomach for all that, you can think of getting into business. Of course, it goes unsaid that the fruits of this kind of efforts in the initial years will be rich and sweet in the years to follow.

In these initial testing years, the fire in your belly will need to keep burning. That is only possible if you have enough passion for the business. This passion will come if you identify the actual value that your business creates for society. If your identified 'value' resonates with what you love, your passion will stay burning for a long time. If the process of creating such value is in line with your own skills or knowledge, the passion will translate into meaningful action. Meaningful action will create desirable results.

 Understand, that you cannot make it big in business if you think about your profits. Think about creating value. Think of solving some real-life problem for someone. Put in the hard work to deliver that value. The money will follow. In the case of e-waste business, it is a great value creator for all stakeholders namely the society, the natural environment, the waste warriors and the government.

e-Waste is definitely toxic if mishandled or simply dumped in a landfill. So by recycling e-waste, you will eliminate a certain amount of toxicity, prevent a large amount of carbon equivalent of emissions, and generally reduce pollution to a large extent. This is a great benefit to society since it causes a direct positive impact on their health or reduces the negative impact of pollution created due to mismanaged or unmanaged e-waste. You can create a positive impact on the entire society at large.

You can recover various metals through e-waste recycling. These recovered metals can be reused in the industry for making new fresh products. This secondary source of metals will result in a lesser demand on primary metal, i.e metal from ore. This, in turn, will reduce mining to a large extent, thereby reducing deforestation and nullify the ill effects of the same. For example, research has shown that gold recovered from 1 ton of mobile phones is equivalent to the amount extracted from 17 tons of gold ore! And to think about it, gold presence is just about 0.003% in cell phone waste. Now if we add other metals that can be recovered such as copper, silver, tin, etc., it would mean a significant amount of ore replacement. So, 1 ton of mobile phone scrap may save a small hill from destruction.

Besides reduced mining, it requires much lesser energy and water to recover metals from e-waste than extract the same from ores. Also, since the metals used in e-waste are usually high grade, they can be used almost directly in most metal applications. So the cost and pollution related to refining are also saved to a large extent.

Now if we add up all the e-waste generated in the country, the equation simply blows out of proportion. And then, think about the saving of trees, conservation of ecosystems, biomes, animal habitats and nature in general, your one e-waste recycling facility can help in conserving a few hundred acres of nature every year, to say the very least.

Third, waste warriors, as I prefer to call them, are the workers in e-waste management space. In informal sector recycling, these waste warriors are subjected to inhuman, unsafe and toxic working conditions. By setting up an organized e-waste recycling facility where workers have a safe and healthy working environment, you can impact their lives and provide them with a dignified living. Besides, the informal e-waste sector usually employs child labour for many tedious tasks. With your organized business, these children can now go to school and create a brighter future for themselves.

Fourth, since metals are recovered from the scrap in your own country, you reduce a significant amount of import of metals. In fact, you can also help in making your country export positive and make a valuable contribution to the economy, exchange rate and help in creating national wealth.

Fifth, by getting into the organized sector, you can be an early mover in this space still in the sun-rise stage as of 2020, thus helping to create a whole new industry through your success. Of course, a new industry will mean those many more jobs, added tax revenue to the exchequer, added GDP, and a host of other macroeconomic benefits.

This one business has the potential of transforming the lives of many people including you.

If creating this kind of value ignites your passion, you can decide to get into the e-waste recycling business. Keep in mind, it is a tough business and not everyone's cup of tea. You will be slogging harder than ever. During one of those days when invariably you will feel like quitting, think about all the value you can create and all the lives that you will be impacting positively and all the money that you would make. That will keep your business alive and kicking. If you can sustain the thunderstorm of the e-waste business for the first 2-3 years, you are sure to land in paradise in the following years.

Action Time

Based on the above thoughts and your own ideas, you may want to answer the 2 extremely important questions.

a. Why do you want to get into a business?

b. Why do you want to get into an e-waste related business?

The answers to these questions will lead you to create your mission and vision statements and identify the underlying values for your business. Remember you are out to create an enterprise and not just another run of the mill scrap trading house. You may still trade in scrap, but it would be at an enterprise scale. It is not about what you do, it is about how you do whatever you do. This is the single thing that will differentiate you and help you build a unique culture in the long run.

This is perhaps the smallest chapter of this book. However, it may end up becoming the biggest and richest chapter of your life!

Chapter 2

Fundamentals of an e-Waste business

What is e-waste?

Any electrical or electronic equipment can be classified as e-waste after it has outlived its useful life. Electrical and electronic equipment usually have a rated life cycle. Most computers and related equipment have a life cycle of 3 years. This is typically the time required for the technology to undergo a change significant enough to render the product obsolete. Usually, the manufacturer's warranty period is considered as the lifecycle of electrical and electronic equipment. Depending on the equipment it may range from 1 year to about 7 years. However, for most of the products, their lifecycle would fall within the 1 to 3 years time frame. Beyond this time, the product is supposed to be replaced by a new one. The older replaced product is what is commonly known as e-waste.

However, in India and many other countries, irrespective of the manufacturer's warranty, the equipment may continue to be in service for a much longer time. This is because of various factors such as the large unorganized technician base, the cultural ethos of stocking old equipment, an expectation of scrap/resale value, etc. Therefore, from this conservative perspective, we must consider the useful life of a product to be as long as it continues to give the service that it was originally intended to give. On an average, in the case of mobile phones, it goes up to 2 to 3 years. In the case of PCs, it may go up to 5 to 6 years, though the warranty typically expires within 1 and 3 years respectively. This extended usage of these types of equipment is predominantly due to reasons such as upgrade, refurbish, repair and reuse, a donation to charity, repurposing, etc. However, this usage life is consistently on the decline and is expected to fall by around 12% year on year.

Everything that uses electricity to run can be classified as electrical or electronic equipment, i.e. EEE. When it goes out of service as mentioned above, it becomes Waste EEE or WEEE. We shall be using this term WEEE and e-waste interchangeably throughout the rest of the book. So everything from your Fitbit band to the main electrical power distribution panel installed in your housing complex can come under WEEE or e-waste. It includes white goods such as washing machines, refrigerators, electric ovens, microwave ovens, television, air conditioners, fans, food processing devices, bulbs, tubes, CD/DVD players, torches, karaoke systems, mobile phones, landline phones, digital cameras, and everything else that you use normally in the household. Other industrial or commercial products such as laptops, PCs, workstations, servers, switches, routers, data centre equipment, storage arrays, backup devices, telecom switching systems, antennas, transmission systems, power backup systems, access control devices, motors, electrical distribution panels, wireless networking devices and everything else that may be used for commercial purposes is a part of e-waste or WEEE.

In manufacturing setups, the classification of e-waste becomes slightly difficult because we have many mechanical machines that use electricity. For example a Lathe machine. Can the entire lathe machine be considered as e-waste? The answer is no. The lathe machine motors, starters, the wiring, control logic board and sensors can come under e-waste. However, as a WEEE operator/processor, you will not get these items removed from the lathe machine before it is scrapped. Hence, you can pick up the entire scrapped machine and record the weight of the specific components that can constitute WEEE as your total collection. Similarly, if we consider a medical device such as an MRI scanner, will it come under e-waste? The answer is yes, it will. However an electronically controlled bed will not come under e-waste; only the motors, actuators, control systems and wiring will be a part of e-waste. However, as mentioned in the case of a lathe machine, you will still need to pick up the whole bed when the hospital scraps it. Same is true for automobiles as well. We shall have a detailed discussion on compositions and classifications of WEEE a little later. As of now, it is clear that anything that uses electrical energy for operation and is now out of service can classify as e-waste.

Where is the hazard in e-waste?

All the above items that we listed as potential candidates for coming in the WEEE stream seem quite benign. So where is the hazard? Why is WEEE called hazardous? And if it is so hazardous, how come we use it from applications like food processing and carry it on our selves as if it is an extended organ of the body?

Electronic items are not at all hazardous while in use (barring some exceptions), if they are simply kept on your tabletop or inside your drawer. (Unless there are batteries inside them). The problem starts when it is scrapped and trashed carelessly. If your dead pen-drive is carelessly dumped along with other waste, it will follow the rest of the trash to a common dumping bin from where it will go all the way to a solid waste dumping ground. When this pen drive comes in contact with heat and humidity, it starts degenerating. Just like iron tends to rust when exposed to humidity or silver tends to blacken or copper tends to turn green, the metals used within the pen-drive also start corroding.

Corrosion is essentially a chemical reaction. Most of you would have seen a leaking dry cell battery. The cell is made up of dry matter. So where does the leakage occur from? The same phenomenon happens when corrosion starts. The metals present in your pen-drive form small ionic cells locally and start an electron exchange, helping in leaching of the metals into the soil or water. Besides, these days we have occurrences of acid rain. In fact, even neutral rainwater when it runs across soil can become acidic or alkaline depending on the type of the soil. These acidic or alkaline environments accelerate metal leaching. These metals leached into the soil form their own compounds which are generally water-soluble and tend to percolate down the topsoil and find their way to groundwater. This is how groundwater may start getting contaminated with arsenic content, sulphates, cyanides and other dangerous or toxic substances.

Another thing is emissions. Some WEEE may emit certain toxic gases when they come in contact with heat or when broken. For example when a CFL bulb breaks, the gases inside the bulb escape in the atmosphere. Mostly it is argon gas and a very little mercury vapour. Argon gas is inert and has no direct adverse environmental impact. However, if a large number of CFLs are broken open in a closed environment, it can lead to a high concentration of argon and cause asphyxiation. Prolonged exposure to such an environment has adverse health impacts such as dizziness, drowsiness, nausea, depression etc. Mercury vapour is toxic by nature and has a strongly adverse health impact on humans as well as other ecosystems and biomes. Mercury and its various forms build inside life tissues over a while before they start showing symptoms such as uneasiness, damage to the nervous system and embryonic developmental problems. Mercury vapours actually undergo changes and eventually transform to methylmercury which is at least 5 times more toxic than elemental mercury.

Frankly, while we all need multiple salts and elements in our normal course of life, excessive exposure to any metal or element has some or the other adverse effects on the human body. Since WEEE is full of metals and other not-so-very-benign non-metals in significantly large concentrations than found naturally, the whole case becomes quite toxic or hazardous. That brings us to the general composition of WEEE.

Composition of e-waste

e-Waste or WEEE comprises of multiple types of material. For example, if we consider a laptop, we have an external plastic casing, the LED or LCD panel, the motherboard, the battery, hard drive and so on. The plastic also varies in terms of quality within different points of origin. For example, the plastic used for the power supplies could be different as compared to the laptop cover. Also, the plastic used for the keys on the keyboards and the plastic used at the hinges could be different. The motherboard has multiple components mounted on it including ICs, heat sinks, MLCCs, etc. Each of these has a specific intrinsic composition. It could contain copper, silver, arsenic, cobalt, gold, silver etc. The display panel uses indium, tin, and silicon dioxide apart from several polymers and polyamides.

While we know the principal components of EEE, it is difficult to identify the level of content with surety. This is because, for every category of EEE, each manufacturer, each model may have different compositions though the equipment may seem the same. For example within PC servers, there are many models and many manufacturers. Each one may have a different composition depending on the specifications and also on the manufacturing SOPs of the particular plant where it is made. To illustrate the point in more detail, let us consider a few ICs and their gold content.

Table 1 : Precious metal content at a component level

Category	Class	Component	Gold Content
CPUs	High Yield CPUs	NEC R10000	0.27 g
		AMD K5	0.4 g
		Pentium Pro	0.3 to 0.5 g
		Cyrix 586	0.25 g
		Intel 486 SX	0.1 g
		Intel 486 DX	0.19 - 0.2 g
	Low Yield CPUs	Intel Celeron	
		Intel Core 2 Duo	Less than 0.05 g
		Intel i3, i5, i7	
		Intel Pentium 2, 3, 4	

Like Gold, there are many other metals in electronic components. As per our independent research, we have identified up to 60 elements in varying quantities present in electronics. However, most of these elements are present only in traces. From a recovery perspective, it is wise to focus on a set of fewer metals and treat the rest of the metals as non-recoverable. Sometimes, in certain specific types of metals, you also get platinum, rhodium etc. However, since the concentration of these elements is low and the occurrence is among a very few components, it may not make sense to even think about putting up a separate process for identifying, isolating and recovery of these metals.

Electrical and Electronic equipment contains a large spectrum of primary metallic and non-metallic elements, alloys and compounds such as Copper, Aluminium, Gold,

Silver, Palladium, Platinum, Nickel, Tin, Lead, Iron, Sulphur, Arsenic, Vanadium, Indium, etc. While many of these elements and compounds are useful to different industries, if left unattended to disintegrate or decompose on their own, they can pose a severe environmental and health hazard as mentioned earlier. It may also be noted that some of the above mentioned (or otherwise) elements are in so minuscule quantities, that it may not be viable to reclaim them both technically as well as commercially.

There is one more way of studying e-waste composition from the point of view of the recycler. As a recycler, you are primarily interested in the recoverable value. Knowing about the hazards is important from a safety perspective. But from a business viability perspective, you would like to know where your money lies.

e-waste collection can be primarily classified as (a) related to consumer durables, (b) related to IT and telecom, (c) industrial and other commercial goods. The proportion of these classes changes from geography to geography depending on their demographics, business concentrations, and other issues. For example, in India, in places such as Bangalore, Chennai, Hyderabad, Gurgaon, Mumbai etc, where you have a large concentration of software companies, BPOs, KPOs, banking and other IT enables services, the IT and telecom related waste generation may be as high as 80% of the entire e-waste. While in other places where the concentration of manufacturing setups is stronger, such as Kolhapur, Ludhiana, etc the industrial waste is much higher to the tune of about 30%. In places where you have a mix of everything (usually these are tier 2 cities) such as Jaipur, Ahmedabad, Surat, Pune, Aurangabad, Nagpur, Kanpur, Indore, Bhopal, Patna, Kolkata, etc the composition is much more balanced with a good proportion of white goods (consumer durables). However, in general, the skew is a bit towards IT and telecom due to the emergence of IT, rapid urbanization and churn of the migrant population, and the emergence of neo rich class. Therefore, it may be a reasonable assumption to consider the primary e-waste categorization as :

Table 2: Average categorization of potential WEEE generation

Collection (Tons)	
IT and Telecom	60%
Non-IT Products	40%

Table 3: Average composition of WEEE (by weight)

Composition of IT&Telecom waste		Composition of Non-IT Waste	
Metal cabinets	**50%**	Metal	**50%**
Plastic + Glass	**10%**	Plastic	**20%**
Circuit boards	**25%**	Circuit Boards	**5%**
Wires	**15%**	Wires	**15%**
		Glass	**10%**

Table 4: Average metal and non-metal composition of PCBs and other parts

PCB and active electronics (30% by wt.)		Casing, castings, Non-EE parts[*] (70% by wt.)	
Copper	16%	Plastic	30%
Gold	0.03%	Ferrous Metal	35%
Silver	0.1%	Aluminium	5%

Palladium	**0.01**	Glass	20%
Lead	**2 %**	Copper	10%
Aluminium	**5 %**	**Total**	**100%**
Iron	**5 %**		
Nickel	**1 %**	*Estimated	
Solder	**0.66 %**		
Epoxy	**58 %**		
Other	**12.2 %**		
Total	**100%**		

Source: *Consolidated data from Various Journals and reports*

Though the above percentages can be understood based on averages, not all types of WEEE need to follow the same. Each lot will differ from each other. Another method of looking at the numbers could be based on the actual demand for metals placed by the EEE manufacturing sector. A study in 2009 shows that the total annual demand for metals from EEE manufacturing in the US alone was worth 45.4 million USD (Schulep, et. al. 2009). In other words, we can say that the worth of metals that may be recoverable from the electronic waste of these US manufacturers after their usable life, on average say 3 years, i.e. in 2012 would have been 45.4 million. In reality, this value was surely lower since not much of recycling happened even in the US in those times and even if the whole lot were to be recycled, it would still be perhaps lesser because all metals need not be recovered due to rational decisions about techno-commercial viability.

In the real world, the major metals that are recovered from EEE are Copper, Iron, Aluminium, Tin, Nickel, Silver, Gold, Platinum, and Palladium. There are other elements such as Lead, Phosphorus, Cobalt, Selenium, Vanadium,

Silicon etc which are present either in traces or are not so valuable or are not recoverable. Other items are plastic and glass. Of all of the metals/non-metals, it may make economic sense to focus on only a few items and the rest of the residue may be sold off to other interested recyclers.

It is therefore impossible to correctly identify and predict the 'economic quality' of e-waste. Secondly, from a recycler's perspective, the collection cannot be restricted to a certain type and quality of equipment. Neither can the collection volume be assured. Unlike a manufacturing setup where the supply of raw material can be guaranteed in terms of time, quantity and quality of supply through contracts, in case of recycling or de-manufacturing, there can be no such assurance. Every single collection batch can differ from the next one drastically in both quantity and quality. Therefore any amount of due diligence in assessing the economic value of the collection can only be as good as any guesswork, which brings us to the question of collection. But before that, let us quickly have a look at current e-waste handling practices.

Action Time

Based on the above understanding, can you now simply list down some points that you feel are good for e-waste business and some that you feel are not so good. You need not consider what is good for you. It is not from your perspective. It should be a simple unbiased opinion about what is generally good or not so good for the e-waste business irrespective of who is doing the business.

Remember, 'not-so-good' does not necessarily mean that it is bad news. It simply means that you need to cover these areas of potential risk.

You can use the following template.

Conducive for e-Waste business	Not so conducive for e-Waste business.

Chapter 3

Current e-Waste handling practices

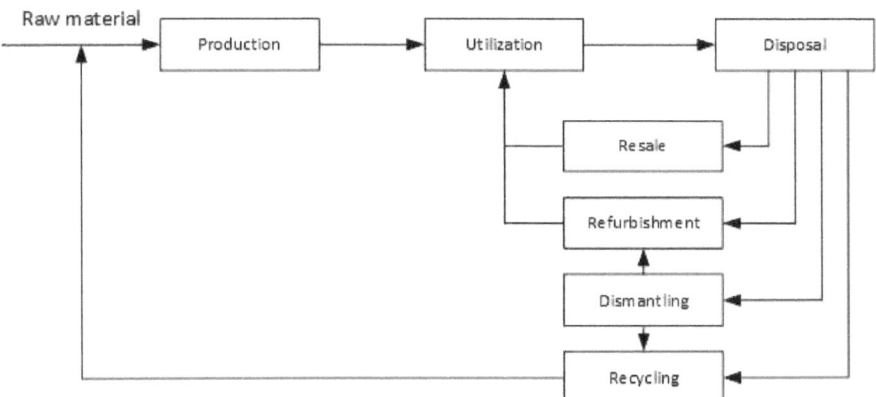

Figure 1: Activity chain of electronics products: manufacturing to disposal (simplified)

E-waste is generated in households and corporates (including private and government companies). In many situations, the defunct EEE does not enter the stream of recycling. Consumers do not dump products even after the end of its useful life.

If you check in your own homes, 9 out of 10 chances are that you would have at least a couple of old phones, calculators, cameras and other small stuff simply lying in your drawers, completely defunct. Why do you think you do not dispose of these items?

This behaviour is partly due to cultural ethos. The tendency of stockpiling WEEE products is high. As per one study 68% of WEEE is stockpiled in the USA (HP, 2005). In India, the number is likely to be much higher. One another reason for this stockpiling behaviour is that consumers expect some value when they dispose of the scrap. They would be willing to dispose of their e-waste only if they get suitable incentives. Many times, this also happens simply because it is too insignificant. Lack of awareness, laziness, and sheer ignorance are other reasons. Perhaps your own answers to the earlier question may give you some more reasons. We can use these reasons to create great collection strategies.

Many Corporate entities also exhibit the stockpiling behaviour of households. However, in the case of business entities, the stockpiling is largely due to procedural hassles involved in selling their assets, especially so if they are exempt from customs duty like as in a case of an SEZ or 100% EOU. In such cases, their equipment is usually imported and therefore is custom bonded. To be able to sell it, there may be a customs duty payable which becomes an additional cost. WEEE from corporate houses many times include usable products, because of their technology refresh policies.

The collection of waste from all these sectors happens in different ways. The collection mechanism is dependent on where the e-waste is generated i.e. in households or corporates.

Collection from households

Depending on the city where they are located, people sell their waste to local scrap dealers who collect the waste from door-to-door. In many places, these scrap dealers also have their own chain of collection through a group of rag pickers. A Scrap dealer usually collects an assortment of different types of waste including e-waste. Another channel of WEEE collection is retail chains. Many retail outlets for electronic consumer goods often float buy-back schemes or exchange programs. However, such programs are seasonal and product-specific. Many types of WEEE do not come under an exchange program. For example, in large format retail stores, buy-back schemes are not available for products like CD/ DVD players while it is available for products like televisions, washing machines, refrigerators, laptops etc.

Collection from corporate business houses

Companies sell their WEEE to second-hand buyers through various means such as auction, scrap sale or open bidding. Many times cumbersome rules force businesses to use unfair means like damaging the products in a conjured accident and then selling to a second-hand buyer. Another way in which business houses get rid of old equipment is by enforcing a buy-back arrangement on technology vendors. In such transactions, usually, there is a channel partner of an OEM involved who takes the old equipment and either resells, cannibalizes or simply stockpiles the same.

Yet another way in which e-waste is collected is through collection points sponsored by NGOs, manufacturers or the businesses themselves as a CSR activity. Individual consumers can dump select e-waste at these collection points. For example, some time back Nokia had arranged boxes in a few corporate offices for the consumers to dump or deposit used phones. I guess most of them are withdrawn now. Though the arrangement was made by Nokia with an objective of collecting old phones for spare cannibalization, building their brand and subtly enticing the customer to buy a new Nokia phone, it did not work. Why?

When was the last time that you deposited your old phone in such a collection bin? Think about what were the reasons. You will be surprised to realise that many times the master strategists or policymakers oversee simple things that you and I can easily spot.

The down streams and side streams

Ragpickers sell their collection from households and dump yards to scrap dealers. Usually, scrap dealers pay for e-waste received based on the weight. Higher the volume sold to scrap dealers, higher is the money earned by the ragpicker. Of course, it is also dependent on how each side bargains. These negotiations are often interesting to hear! So next time you see a rag picker standing near a roadside scrap traders shop, try to listen to their exchange and you will have a field day! Just beware not to make your interest too obvious.

Retailers, after collecting e-waste using buy-back schemes, may resell the products if it is usable or resend it to the respective manufacturer or sell to scrap dealers. Second-hand buyers may resell the products or donate to NGOs etc.

if it is usable. Else, it is cannibalized or sold to scrap dealers.

Manufacturers, after collecting e-waste through their collection points or via retailers, can use as many parts or materials as they can for manufacturing new products. However, most manufacturers do not have an organized method for reuse of spares. A more common situation is that spares are cannibalized and stocked by service providers of various types of equipment. Parts and materials that cannot be used further are either stocked in warehouses or sold to scrap dealers. Manufacturers not having the capability to reuse parts and materials in their new products, may sell the e-waste to recyclers.

Nowadays in India, the regulations have started becoming a little stricter and hence institutions usually sell their WEEE only to authorized recyclers/dismantlers/collection agents. However, the informal sector continues to be very strong in India and other developing countries.

The informal sector

Most of the recycling community works in the informal sector. In this sector, the collection is completely manual and from the doorstep of the generator. A collector usually does not differentiate in the WEEE types. This aggregate WEEE is taken by a larger scrap dealer who does the value-added activity of segregation into classes or categories. For every type of waste, there is a further classification based on whether the product is still usable and whether it has market demand. This decision is completely based on the scrap dealer's best judgment. The non-usable equipment is then dismantled manually.

The easily separable parts such as plastics, glass, metal cabinets etc are directly sold in various markets. The more complicated parts such as motherboards, assemblies, fused parts etc are sometimes sold to a recycler who is usually from the informal sector.

The traditional informal recycler uses crude techniques such as open burning or acid leaching to separate metals. These metals are sold to smelters further higher up in the value chain. In most cases, the extraction techniques are so crude that the output is also contaminated. Also, the efficiency of such techniques is only about 30%. Besides the environmental damage is beyond imagination.

From the usable part of the collected WEEE, some are sold directly in second-hand sale, some are refurbished and sold as a refurbished product, some is donated to charity and some are rented. Of these 4 methods, the first is the most popular for the simple reason of the quick cash turnaround and no requirement of supporting infrastructure in the form of refurbishing processes or post-sale support.

Assessing the exact proportion of reuse, refurbishing, and recycling of collected WEEE is almost impossible to arrive at with certainty. It completely depends on the due diligence, capability and opportunity available with the collector at that point in time. However, on an average based on certain unstructured surveys conducted among generators of waste, we understand that depending on the generator, on an average about 25-30% of WEEE gets reused or refurbished.

Socio-economic factors

Among households, depending on their economic strata the tendency to junk old equipment changes. Usually, WEEE collected from upper economic classes is reusable, that collected from the upper-middle class is refurbishable or directly reusable and that collected from the lower middle class is recyclable.

Similarly, WEEE generated within large MNCs, large Indian IT-savvy companies is usually reusable or refurbishable, that generated within large and medium Indian companies is usually refurbishable or recyclable and that generated within small companies is definitely recyclable. Also, most of the usable WEEE generated from large MNCs ends up being auctioned/sold among their own staff. This portion of the WEEE in its later lifecycle follows the general distribution pattern for household generated scrap.

Some portion of usable WEEE from all corporate is donated to NGOs or schools or other such institutions. Again this portion follows the general pattern of small companies.

Figure 2 on the next page explains the entire lifecycle of e-waste in India with reference to various possible starting points. Irrespective of where the electronic goods become classified as scrap, essentially they find their way to a scrap dealer. Once the material reaches a scrap dealer, the next steps are predictable.

Figure 2 :e-Waste life cycle : current scenario

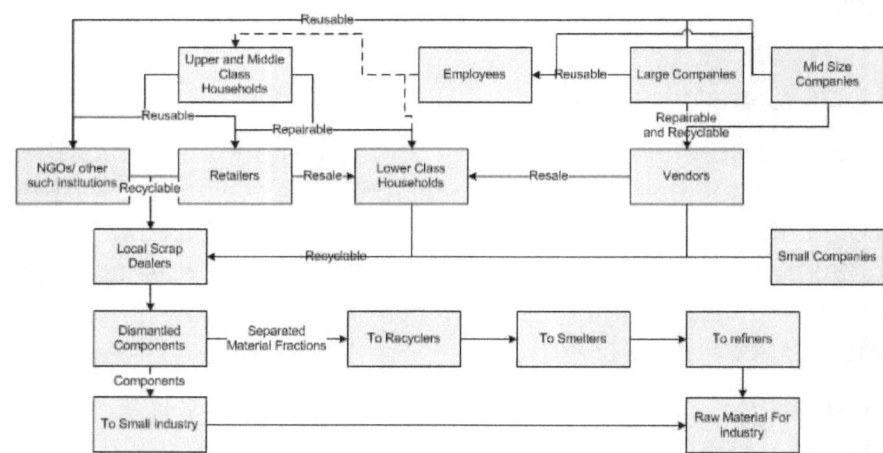

The entire complexity and unpredictability lie in the consumption/waste generation stage.

Action Time

So can you now do a simple task of listing down what all are the areas where you can play a role? Think based on the flowchart shown in figure 2. Where are the possible bottlenecks? Can you do something to solve the problem and create value? What resonates with you the most?

Of course, this book will outline a complete business model for end-to-end recycling. However, it is not necessary to do everything in the chain. You can also build your business on any single link of the value chain. Just make sure that the link is vital to the chain so that you become a valuable part of the ecosystem.

As of now, let us simply restrict to finding areas of potential value creation. You can perhaps do a brainstorming exercise with some of your friends to list down these value creation points. We shall use them later in the next chapter after we do a general market analysis and take an overview of the business environment and its impacting forces.

Chapter 4

Market analysis for setting up an e-waste management business

There are many ways of analysing a market. I think it is crucial in the modern days to think about every business from the customer-centric perspective. Gone are the days where businesses were built based on a product or technology USP. Unique selling proposition is no more enough. We need a unique value proposition. It is not about sales anymore. Relevant value creation, competitive edge and comparative advantage are the new tenets of a successful business.

So when you think about creating a relevant value, you need to know your customer. We have already seen some part of customer behaviour in the previous chapter. We need to perhaps delve into some more details. So who is your customer when you think about e-waste?

Customer

For an e-Waste management business is a customer profile is quite complex. The buyer and the seller are both your potential customers. For example, on one side, there is the traditional second-hand buyer who buys the repaired/refurbished products. On the other side, this same buyer is also likely to become a seller later who would need to be addressed very differently to ensure that he gives the

WEEE back to you and not to another e-waste recycler. While the person may be the same, his needs and points of concern are different when he is a buyer and when he becomes a seller. He must see a value that is relevant to him depending on the phase that he is in. Hence we need to consider different strategies for tackling both.

In another scenario, if you are a pureplay recycler recovering metals from WEEE and are not engaged in resale or refurbishing, you may want to identify a metal commodity exchange as a customer or directly sell metals as raw material to different industry segments that require these metals. On the supply side, you may need to work closely with the bulk waste generators, PROs, other informal sector operators, the domestic sector and so on. In this case, the entities are different and hence the way they see value is also different.

Buyers

The typical output of an e-Waste recycler is in the form of resale or refurbished equipment, rental equipment, shredded fractions of various materials with differing degrees of separation and recovered metals. The buyers of all of these products are different.

The buyers of second hand refurbished products have a clear need for easy access to the shopfront, low price, good quality of service and an easy upward migration path. Hence if you are well versed with sales and support of electronic products, this makes good sense for you. Else, you will need to set up a complete structure for this business. Some of the potential buyers are the technology users either in the startups, corporate or household space. With newer business models and transaction methods coming up, this is not a very big challenge. However, if you are already in that kind of business, it is much easier for you. Otherwise, it may be beneficial to focus on some other link in the value chain.

If you are planning to be a recycler and work in the area of metal recovery, you would do well to focus clearly on separating the fractions and reclaiming the metals and non-metals contained in the e-waste. Your buyers would mainly be smelters, plastic recyclers, glass recyclers, metal traders, metal buyers, metal product manufacturers, metal exchanges etc. In their case, they seek value in the quality of your product and consistency of supply. Price is always a part of a business transaction. But if you are competing against fresh metal, you always have an edge. If you are competing with another recycler, you will need to find an area of specialization and differentiate yourself to create a unique value.

Suppliers

As we know from the earlier chapter, the suppliers could be both household and corporate entities. But while they are both supplying the same item i.e. WEEE, their needs or the way they would want to conduct business will differ significantly. Business houses may not necessarily look at maximum realization from the sale of WEEE. It is not their core business and the bottom-line impact that such scrap sale will possibly have on their balance sheet is likely to be negligible. In fact, their cost of holding inventory and conducting prolonged negotiations may be higher than the incremental realization that they may hope for. However, needless to say, it is in human nature to maximize their share of the spoils! Usually, many business houses may conduct an auction to get rid of their e-scrap. It may be a closed or open auction depending on their choice. Usually, it is a quick, closed auction.

You may also possibly get into contractual agreements with business houses. But the contract will never guarantee you a quantity or quality of supply. At best, the customer may simply declare that you will be the preferred or one of the preferred vendors for selling their WEEE. You may want to maintain great relationships with the person in the materials and warehouse management role.

Household WEEE can be collected through a network of scrap dealers, retail outlets, innovative doorstep campaigns, digital apps etc. OEMs can also be large suppliers or at least may be great vehicles for mobilizing a supply chain. We shall talk about collections in a separate chapter. After all, an efficient and effective collection mechanism is one of the main elements of a profitable e-Waste recycling business.

When we are trying to understand the market, it is not enough to know only about the customers. Your competition is an essential part of the market ecosystem. And contrary to what you may feel, competition is essential for a business to survive. If the competition is high, it means that the business has a lot of potential and will last for a long time. If there is no competition, you need to ask some critical questions to yourself. Luckily in e-waste recycling, there is a tough competition, though most of it is from the informal sector.

Competition

While the informal sector is the biggest competitor, it has several systemic weaknesses which you can take advantage of. As of 2020, WEEE regulations are still nascent in India. As the e-waste regulations become more stringent over the years and overall awareness increases, this scenario is likely to change with most government and business entities preferring to do business based on contracts with the organized sector. We have already witnessed a significant change over the last few years in India.

Within the organized sector, the competition is still weak. As of January 2020, there were only about 150 odd registered recyclers in India. Total installed capacity is about 200000 tons i.e just about 10% of the overall volume generated annually! This means there is room for about 1000 – 1500 more recycling units and a potential of about 150 additional every year. In most developing countries the scenario is more or less the same. In fact, in developed countries also, the recycling infrastructure is not sufficient and there is enough room for an aspiring entrepreneur to set shop there if he has the necessary resources.

Market Size

Accurate market analysis for e-waste management is very difficult primarily because there are too many variables. In the opening chapter on e-waste fundamentals, we saw that equipment lifecycles change based on demographics of the local population.

However, based on an unstructured dipstick survey that I had conducted sometime back, I found that most Indian households have a predictable usage cycle for appliances. For example, typical usage cycle for washing machines is 6 years, that for television sets (CRT) is typically 8-9 years, that for refrigerators and ACs is averagely 10 years and that for cellphones is generally 1-2 years. Also, the latest observation is that the typical usage cycles of white goods are also coming down due to the burgeoning middle class, the neo rich in India and the increased affordability of electronics.

For arriving at the growth potential of the business, you can look at the numbers reported by electronic goods manufacturers. All of them seem to be growing at about 6-8 % year on year in terms of turnover. In terms of units, this could be about 8-10%. All of this sale at some time will flow in the WEEE stream.

Table 5: e-Waste market size in India

Year	e-Waste Generated	Processed by Organized Sector	Processed by informal sector (Estimated)
2005	146,800 MTA	7000 MTA	125,000 MTA
2008	332,000 MTA	15000 MTA	250,000 MTA
2009	440,000 MTA	19000 MTA	350,000 MTA
2010	600,000 MTA	28000 MTA	420,000 MTA
2011	800,000 MTA	50000 MTA	450,000 MTA
2012	1,000,000 MTA	65000 MTA	450,000 MTA
2013	1,200,000 MTA	120000 MTA	460,000 MTA
2014	1,300,000 MTA	150000 MTA	460,000 MTA

2015	1,370,000 MTA	180000 MTA	460,000 MTA
2016	1,700,000 MTA	200000 MTA	480,000 MTA
2017	2,100,000 MTA	?	?
2020	7,500,000 MTA	?	?

Note: These numbers are an average from various credible sources. The numbers of organized and the informal sector do not tally with the total generation. This may mean that the remaining portion has been stockpiled or is under reuse. This portion will eventually land back in the recycling stream. (2014 onwards the data is not verified but obtained from trustworthy sources)

The above table clearly indicates that the amount of e-waste generated in India is increasing roughly around 20-25% YoY. With the middle class growing in size and purchasing power, the consumption of electronic goods will only increase and therefore lead to more e-waste being generated.

Chart 1 : e-Waste generation rate in India

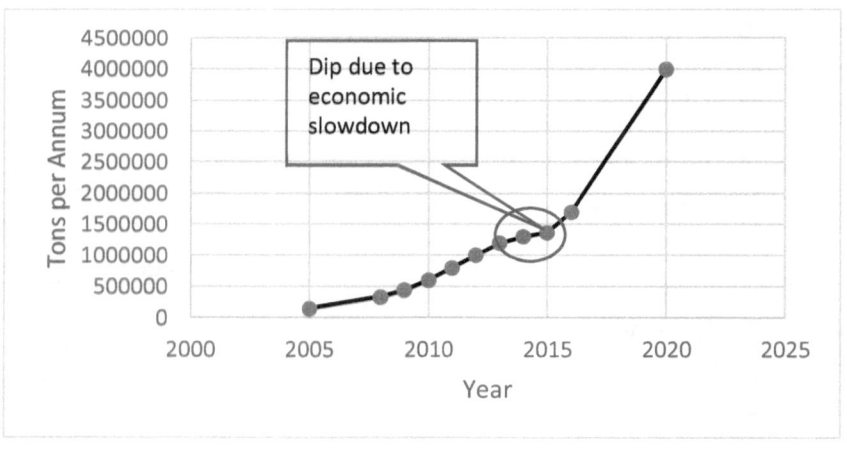

Some interesting facts about Indian e-waste environment

India has an interesting blend of urban (~15%), semi-urban(~30%) and rural (~55%) population. Given the size of our population, any fraction of any demographic unit is a large chunk in itself.

- PC penetration in India is estimated to be 90 per 1000 as compared to 997 in the US. This shows the immense potential for the refurbished PC market. Most of the untapped market is at the bottom of the pyramid where cost is an issue. Refurbishing can solve this cost problem driving PC penetration quite high.

- High technology penetration in Urban areas (>70%). This means that the highest source of e-waste is here. It, however, does not give any measure of how much of the technology penetration is with new products versus old products. The unique nature of Indian urban demographics suggests that there is a sizeable market for refurbished goods.

- Moderate penetration in semi-urban areas but a high growth rate(~100%). Semi-urban areas have rather confusing demographics. The users here are brand-conscious, price-conscious, interested in technology and represent a large ambitious and upwardly mobile mass.

- Very low rural penetration and medium growth rate, but accelerating very fast. This is the majority of the "bottom of the pyramid" market who is willing to readily absorb anything new and affordable. This is the hinterland full of opportunities that are largely untapped due to the logistical difficulties of reach and services.

- Large companies refresh PCs every 4 years(avg). Most companies force a buyback on unwilling vendors. Buyback material goes partly in captive reuse (<10%), partly in rental (about 30%), partly deadstock (almost 40%) and partly disposed to the local *kabadi*. Transactions only fetch "distress sale values". This is primarily because these vendors are primarily interested in the fresh sale and have no real use of old stuff.

- E-waste business potential is projected to be at USD 5.4 Billion in FY 2020 as per Markets and Markets.

- In India, organized e-Waste recycling is a nascent industry.

All these factors make the e-waste market a high potential one and very unique in various ways. Besides these insightful points, there are very obvious points such as global pressures to promote green businesses, legislative drafts being circulated within the government circles, heavy subsidies declared by the governments, tax holidays, global e-waste processing regulations taking shape, etc.

Global Outlook

In many developing countries such as India, an informal network of waste processors employs techniques such as open burning. Modern recycling facilities are equipped with technologies that can handle these processes with minimal risks to the environment and worker health, while also ensuring the added environmental benefit of optimal recovery of materials. These treatment methods, however, are capital intensive and lend themselves to economies of scale. Financial constraints for electronics recycling prevent the construction and operation of a state-of-the-art facility in all countries. Therefore, though the Basel convention provides against exporting WEEE, there are rampant cases of import under a different classification. Worldwide, therefore negotiations are going on to regularise transboundary movements and the flow of e-waste to certified WEEE recyclers.

With such regulations likely to come up very soon, the preferred countries for e-waste recycling industry are projected to be India and some Latin American and African countries. Such WEEE recycling will be entrusted only to those recyclers who can prove that they can manage WEEE in an environmentally sound fashion. Mechanisms are being worked out for a system of rating and certifying such setups in various countries who may consider this as an opportunity of leading new industry.

Within India, the import of e-waste is still a debated issue and the several conflicting laws add to the confusion. As per the hazardous waste handling rules, e-waste can be imported in India provided it is done so for the purpose of recycling by an authorized recycler who has the supporting infrastructure for carrying out the recycling activity in an environmentally friendly method. The process for this is currently being made easy for compliance and control. However, as of January 2020, e-waste imports are not open in India.

Influencing power of the market forces

Having understood the different market forces and realized certain facts, you would now be wondering whether any of these market forces can influence your business and make you submissive to them. For a businessman, freedom to operate and scale is critical. I am sure you would like to check whether your suppliers or customers and any other entity will be a position to arm-twist you.

Influencing power of buyers

The output of e-waste resposal is in the form of primary metals, the demand for which is ever increasing. The supply of primary metals is under severe constraints due to diminishing production from mines and the increasing difficulty in new mining activities due to the global environmentalist activities. An organized sector e-waste recycling activity clearly fits in this scenario where it can address this demand-supply gap. There is no real threat of substitutes for primary metals due to scarcity and price. Also, the prices of primary metals are fairly transparent and one single buyer or a group of buyers cannot have much impact on the price. All these factors together ensure a weak buyer influence over the industry. And that is good news. Buyers cannot dictate your selling price. It is a perfectly free market.

Influencing power of suppliers

Since the amount of e-waste is increasing and the growth rate of the informal sector tapering off, the supplier will need to work more and more with the organized sector for recycling of e-waste. Furthermore, the cost of stocking WEEE is rising spirally due to increased warehousing costs as well as the unprecedented and sustained rate of growth in its generation. Regulatory obligations force the generators of WEEE to give it only to registered recyclers in the organized sector. All these factors ensure that the suppliers of WEEE cannot have a heavy influence on the industry. That is another piece of good news.

Influencing power of competitors

While some of the informal sector players are trying to shift over to the organized sector, there are high entry barriers due to stringent compliances required to be met which may not be possible despite having investment capacity. For example, an urban recycler handling large volumes in a slum area cannot suddenly set up an authorised recycling facility in the same area due to regulatory issues.

Many new players are likely to come into the business, however, the market is large enough for many more players. Also, the market growth itself can take care of the increasing competition.

The informal sector has an established practice of e-waste collection. However, the chains are very unreliable and fragile. The organized sector has the opportunity to beat the informal recyclers by establishing unique models and methods for collection and reverse logistics to ensure collection of their share of e-waste regularly. Such specific collection engines developed by the early starters in their addressable geographies will act as entry barriers for those entering later. The technology of recycling is also undergoing rapid evolution and that itself can act as a comparative advantage of the organized sector over the informal one. Since technology is capital intensive, the small informal recycler cannot afford the same. Fundraising is not easy for the informal sector because of their illegal status and the "cash" nature of their business. All these factors ensure that while there may be competition from the informal sector, it will eventually fade away or will transform into a supply chain feeding into the organized sector recycling industry.

Competition from the organized players, existing and new ones is not a matter of concern since the market size is sufficient to absorb all of them and more. Also, an early starter can create a comparative advantage for himself through capturing specific niche markets, streamlining the processes and covering the learning curve faster, expanding his capacities and through economies of scale and scope. All these factors clearly say that competition will be there due to the high profitability of the sector. However, it is not a market skewing force.

Government's influencing power

While governments worldwide are obviously the largest influencers in a potentially global industry, they along with global environmental activists are working in favour of organized e-Waste resposal.

Thus from as an industry that faces weak influencing pressures from buyers and suppliers, strong favourable forces from the government sector, systemic weaknesses in competition and exploding market growth, the e-waste recycling space is one of the most attractive industries to get into.

Action Time

So let us get into action. Based on the points of value addition that you jotted down at the end of the earlier chapter and the various market-related aspects that you understood in this chapter, can you now make a simple SWOT analysis for yourself?

Think about that specific area in the entire e-waste ecosystem that you thought you could create value. From the point of view of that area, think about what are your strengths and weaknesses. Based on the market analysis that we have seen above, think over what opportunities does the market present to you. And from the point of view of the same market, think about what could be the possible threats for your business.

You may have to do this independently for each of the value creation areas that you listed down in the last chapter.

You may use the following template.

Strengths	Weaknesses
Opportunities	Threats

When you complete this exercise, you will know which is that single value creation area that you should stick to. Depending on your attitude and aptitude, you may choose based on where you see yourself the strongest or where you see least weaknesses, or where you see the maximum opportunities or where you see maximum strengths or any combination.

Chapter 5

e-Waste: core issue – the collection

By now you would have realized that e-waste collection is the primary challenge. Though the generation of e-waste is about 2 million tons in India (as published by various agencies in 2020), it may still be a challenge to collect 2000 tons for your business every year. But no worries. Let us think about this problem as the same as a sales problem. Let us say you were to manufacture all types of electronics. How would you sell your products in the face of the existing competition? Challenging?

The only difference in e-waste is that this challenge is at the beginning of the process rather than at the end. A typical manufacturing business fights for acquiring customers who would buy their products. An e-waste recycling business fights for acquiring customers who are willing to sell/give away their WEEE. So essentially you are still approaching the same customer. You are still appealing him to do business with you. In the manufacturer's scenario, you are trying to satisfy a certain set of his needs. In the e-waste scenario, you are still trying to satisfy another set of his needs.

So essentially you need to do all those things that you would do in selling for procurement, just that they need to be done differently. The key to ideate and create some strategies about collection is to understand the sellers set of needs. As mentioned in the earlier chapters, you have 2 distinct set of sellers – the household and the institutional seller. There are certain important differences in both these sectors.

We need to think of collecting from the household sector as a corollary to setting up a retail sales business. In a retail sales business, your buyers are individuals. They are the sole decision-makers. Hence decisions are quick. At the same time, each sale is a small ticket size. The number of sale transactions is plenty. Well, we assume that it is a profitable retail business. So the number of transactions better be plenty! You have to attract these individual customers to your shop through certain techniques like discounts, promotional schemes, exchange offers, marquee events etc. In the same way, for e-waste collection, you need to approach these customers with various schemes that create a value proposition for them. Your individual collection lots will be small, so you will need to play the volume game. The question is how. Here are some tips and tricks.

Let us understand that no consumer buys an electronic gadget based on the resale price that it will fetch when he doesn't need it any more. He simply buys it for the value it promises. Once the value is derived, the equipment becomes useless and redundant for him or her. Now when they want to dispose of it, it simply presents them an opportunity to monetize the now redundant product and therefore it becomes very easy for an e-waste buyer to offer a price and buy it out. This is the fundamental reason why e-waste gets traded.

The seller generally has no specific notion of the scrap sale price and he/she will typically try to ask for a little more than what you originally offer to pay. That is the fundamental nature of humans. Sometimes, for working equipment, this may not be necessarily true, but obviously, there is no clear price valuation formula. It is simply based on the whim of the buyer and the seller both.

However, this is what makes the e-waste market so difficult. Bulk e-Scrap is traded anywhere between 10 Rs per kg to 40 Rs per kg. There have been instances when the asking price has gone up as high a 55 to 60 Rs per kg. When it is sold in units, as is done commonly done in the household sector it is usually a flat price with no method of knowing the right valuation. So can you use this to your benefit?

Also, to think about it, the household consumer is now becoming increasingly aware of the environmental problems and climate change issues. He is keen to play some role in reducing pollution but has no idea how to do it. Can you think about a way to capitalize on this factor when transacting with this customer? For example, in a large housing society, you can arrange for an e-waste awareness camp. In the same camp, you can provide a facility for the residents of the society to dispose of their e-waste against a small token gift coupon. It could be tickets of a matinee show, food discount coupons or a loyalty point coupon or anything similar. The sellers will see value in that. Let me caution you, you need to ensure that you don't overpay in the form of coupons. Also, beware that there will be people who would still want cash. However, once you have run the environmental awareness program and communicated the hazards of e-waste and told them about how you do recycling and ensure pollution-free processes, chances are good that they will not mind giving you their e-waste a bit more willingly. This is a tedious exercise. But if you do it for a few times in a residential complex, it will eventually become a ritual and the entire complex can become your home ground for collection.

For corporate e-scrap generators, generally, they may get into an auction mode. However, more often than not, they will insist on a recycler's certificate of disposal as mandated by the e-waste disposal rules. As an authorised recycler, you can use this to your advantage. Many times the informal sector uses someone else's recycling certificate against a small fee to the actual registered recycler. You can highlight this to the institutional seller so that he is aware of such malpractice and generally refrain from conducting business with such a person. Price will surely play a role. However, it is not always necessary that the price will win.

Even for corporate houses, you can offer them some unique propositions under their CSR. For example, if they have a CSR initiative in education, you can tell them to route their e-waste to rural schools through you. That way, you will get a small fee from the school and also have a claim over the goods once they get defunct or are ready for disposal/change. What all such initiatives can you think of?

It may be easy perhaps to think of various such ways of creating a value perception in the minds of people. However, the even more difficult part is to reach to them. You may run magnificent super innovative schemes. But your buyers need to be aware of these schemes. That is where the role of sales and marketing will come.

You will need to create a brand perception in the minds of your target customer base. Creation a brand perception is a continuous exercise. You need to keep hammering on the customer's mind about your existence, and the value that you contribute to them. Digital media is one important media that you cannot ignore. Set up a web site, a Facebook page, linked in page, twitter handle, Instagram account and any other social media popular within your target market. Keep posting your branded content on the same. Ensure that you get the target market to follow you. You may need to do a door to door campaign for ensuring this. A simple method of reaching to every house is to run this campaign through schools. School children are great social thinkers! They are generally more environmentally aware and alert than parents. So if we run a campaign in schools to promote your Facebook page, you can rest assured that at least one of the child's parent will like your page and start following you. You may do well to provide some useful content for the children so that they keep continuously following you. Help them create a community. Help them in their school projects related to the environment.

You can run school and college-level competitions on e-waste collection, essays on e-waste, seminars, workshops and even arrange for factory visits for them. This will help to engage very effectively with your audience.

You can create an app for e-waste collection. This app itself can be monetized in many ways adding a significant revenue stream to your business. Can you think of all the ways in which this app can be monetized? One way is local advertisements. There are many more ways.

Spreading awareness is a funny activity sometimes. You can simply have a branded pickup vehicle of your own and keep driving it frequently at strategic timings within your target market. You need not bother whether it has any payload to carry or not. Treat the fuel cost as your marketing expense. Can you think of such methods?

Apart from corporate and household consumers at one end of the spectrum, you have the manufacturer and retailers of electronic goods at the other end. With the extended producer responsibility bill that has come in force, you can decide to focus on building contractual relationships with manufacturers such as Samsung, Nokia, Videocon, HP, IBM, DELL, Cisco, Lucent, Dlink etc. Under the EPR rule, they are mandated to take back their old products. Since most of these companies do not want to get into it, they ask their empanelled vendors to do the collection on their behalf. This is a very big chunk of business. You can work on their behalf as a producer responsibility outsourcing organization. So you can now collect e-waste and pass on the costs to them in a legal way so that they can now cover their EPR obligations. This will also mean an additional source of revenue to fund collections.

The way it works is that if you are a registered recycler, you are authorized to collect any type of scrap depending on the collection capacity cap mentioned on your registration certificate. For example, let us say you have collected 1000 tons of e-waste from various sources. And let us say you have an EPR fulfilment contract with an electronic goods manufacturing company who has an EPR target of say 300 tons. You can simply ask them to fund the cost of 300 tons of collection. You can allocate 300 tons from your collection of 1000 to the EPR contract. The remaining 700 tons can also be attributed to any other manufactures with whom you may have the EPR signed. Physically there are no movements of goods. It is actually another adaptation of the carbon credits trading method.

Apart from that, once empanelled, you can obviously bid for the scrap created through wastages, quality rejections and product obsolescence.

You can work closely with service centres. Repair service is a large business in countries like India. There are multiple small repair centres, both company authorized and privately run. These service centres generate a lot of scrap which you can acquire as an authorised e-waste recycler. As a service centre, they can also work on your behalf as collection points. You can decide on the commercial engagement in such a case.

Get yourself registered as a scrap collection vendor with the Government bodies. The Government is usually the single largest source of scrap. Once empanelled, it becomes a regular affair with different bodies and departments of the government. Of course, it is almost always through a tender. But the quantities are huge.

You can get into a structured relationship with business houses such as banks, software companies, BPOs etc. for being their WEEE recycling partner. These companies regularly run technology upgrades as mandated by their internal rules. The best part is that usually, their WEEE is all in good usable condition. You can sell it off to their own staff immediately on procurement. This reduces your transport cost and frees up a lot of your cash. In fact, if you can sell off about 25% of the total collection, it can help you to cover the cost of the rest. And obviously, once this second-hand machine becomes really obsolete, it comes back to you.

If you find e-waste collection too tedious and are looking for helping hand, you can tie up with NGOs. Many NGOs working in the environmental space are willing to do the collection for an authorised recycler for a minimal fee. All they will need to be assured of is a pollution-free process. You can always take them to your facility to show them the process and get their mind share. Once a particular NGO starts working for you, there will be others who will start talking as well. This can significantly reduce your cost of collection. Besides, the same NGOs can also become your potential customer for refurbished WEEE.

Yet another innovative model could be creating self-help groups of rag pickers. This field force has a door to door approach. Converting them from an unidentified ragpicker to a branded waste worker can create wonders in the reverse logistics space. You can create a huge awareness and momentum simply by giving them a uniform. You can also provide them microfinance for scrap procurement either yourself or through a microfinance company. This will ensure their loyalty. Branded hand carts with special arrangement for elementary classification of WEEE will also help a lot. This does not cost too much and you can be assured of a continuous daily trickle of waste which will add up to a significant amount throughout the year.

You can run regular collection drives in targeted areas such as gated communities, campuses, industrial areas etc. To keep your transport utilization at the optimal level, you may have predecided dates for e-waste collection. For example, in a particular locality, you can schedule your vehicle to visit every 15 days. So each locality is visited twice a month. This may be convenient for the residents also since they have a clear pickup calendar available.

You can also encourage the users to dispose of some types of e-waste through their offices. These offices may be provided with a branded collection bin. Thus, the collection may be streamlined and the bins can be emptied when full. Of course, this will not work with large format goods.

Traditional advertising and newspaper advertorials can have a large impact. However, this is a very expensive proposition. But if you are working with an electronics goods manufacturer for the EPR, you can run a joint advertisement funded by them. It can have a great positive impact on their sales as well. Their regular product ads can also have a small mention of your e-waste pickup service on their behalf. It can be a win-win proposition.

These and many more measures including changes at the policy level by the government can be taken for effective collection. Influencing government policies is a long drawn and time-consuming affair. However, you can time some of your campaigns to coincide with key announcements by the government. That will give a good reach and visibility.

Action Time

Make a list of all the possible segments of your target market within the domestic space. The segmentation should be done based on common customer behaviour. For example, school children can be a segment. Senior citizens can be another.

Similarly, make a list of all Commercial customers within your target geography and segment them in some logical way. Could be based on location or business type or the number of employees.

For each of these segments, think about various ways in which you can reach them.

For each of these segments, list down all the things that they may find value in.

Put it all together to create a market plan. Keep in mind, you should not be incurring huge costs for all this.

You can use the following points -

Customer segment :

Common behavioural traits :

Physical location :

Watering holes : (Where do these people generally hang around)

Possible ways of reaching them :

What is their definition of 'value'?

How do you communicate value to them?

What is the value they can bring to you?

Cost of reach out :

You may decide to skip a few questions or add many more questions. Just ensure that you do not get entangled into too many data points. Else too much of analysis may be counterproductive.

Chapter 6

e-Waste business models

Towards the end of chapter 3, we identified several points where you thought you could add value. You can practically build a business based on that single value creation idea. However, this being a comprehensive e-waste recycling book, let us look at the project holistically.

Like in any other business the key components are supply chain, core process and sales.

Within all the three stages the maximum complexity lies in the supply chain, i.e e-waste collection. But by this time you have already solved the most complex of the issues. At the end of the last chapter, you would have listed down many methods of collection. Supply chain problem being taken care of, we now need to look at the core processes.

The Processing piece is quite complex from a technology perspective. However, with state of the art processing plants, the entire complexity can be made completely transparent. Though fully automated plants are available, the best efficiency in terms of price-performance or in terms of cost recovery is achieved when we have a blend of automation with human intervention. The efficiency of a machine coupled with the intelligence and diligence of a human operator provides the best combination required for maximum accuracy of material separation.

The last piece of the basic process is selling the products of the processed e-waste. There are 3 categories of products, first being resalable equipment, the second being shredded fractions of different material that can be recycled in furnaces or smelting plants and the third is the separated individual metals depending on the investment and the business model chosen. The reusable equipment is refurbished so that its usable life is increased and then resold in the BOP markets. The challenge here is to be able to tap the BOP markets effectively in such a way so that the pricing of the product does not bloat due to distribution and post-sale service costs. The shredded fractions or individual metals are recycled to serve as the raw material for the next production cycle.

Business Model 1: Level 1 (L1) process

This is the very basic model in the e-waste business. You collect the e-waste directly from the waste generators. You can classify the collection into working equipment for resale to end-users. Rest of the WEEE will undergo a further classification based on the nature of the equipment and the method of dismantling the same. For example, CRT monitors and TFT screens are grouped together, Refrigerators and ACs are grouped together, food processors, microwaves, convection ovens are grouped together and so on.

This classified material then enters the second phase of the pre-processing stage, i.e dismantling. Since this is an entry-level model, we have restrictions on budgets. Hence we resort to manual dismantling using simple 'screw-driver-technology".

In the pre-processing stage, we recommend manual dismantling and separation of large parts (For example, cabinets, plastic enclosures and casings, cables, PCBs, Microprocessors, Ram Chips etc). You can now sort out the dismantled parts and sell them separately to prospective buyers. The finer your classification, the higher is your realization. This is because careful classification contributes towards the enrichment of the processed material due to homogeneity and increases the output quality and reduces the cost of the further downstream processing.

If you can, you may further separate the dismantled parts to a component level. Since different components have different compositions, the best practices for recovering their basic elements are different. Carefully classified individual components will realize even more value for you. Remember, we said in the previous chapter that we need to think completely reverse while recycling. In manufacturing, the more complex the product, the higher is the price. However, this complex product when scrapped will realize better value after it is stripped down and simplified!

This business model is very simple and requires the least machinery, lesser space and therefore very low capital. You can start the business with an investment of as low as 5-7 Lakhs INR for equipment and tools. This business model is good if you have limited ambitions. It is not very scalable since it is completely people dependent. It is a good business model until you hit about 250-300 tons of collection per year. Beyond that, you will still do well, but you would tend to realize less money per ton if you do not scale up the business to the next level.

Business Model 2: Level 2 (L2) process, basic

Model 2 is an extension of model 1. You simply add a few processes, put in some machinery, automate a few steps and increase your capacity of processing e-waste. Essentially you still do the same initial processes. In this model, the component level dismantling is no longer a choice. If you do not do it, you will lose money. Also, since the collection has now reached beyond 250-300 Tons per annum, manual component removal becomes too expensive and time-consuming. You will need to invest in some machinery for this purpose.

Since you are now collecting a decent quantity, you now need to also go to the next level in terms of process. You can select some of the assorted parts for copper and aluminium recovery and sell the rest of the parts.

This Level 2 process obviously requires more machinery and enables the dismantler to recover some embedded metals with dry technologies. Selected components after the L1 process are batch fed into a recycling plant assembly. The operation from this point is semi-automated. The salable output is in the form of copper or aluminium powder, flakes or granules depending on the input material.

Typically this model becomes viable after you cross about 300 tons per annum. It can easily scale up to about 2000 tons per annum. Of course, the scalability will depend on your machinery as well. However, if you are thinking that you would install large-sized machinery and that will last you longer, be warned about this. Never buy machinery that will be utilized anything less than 60%. Since mechanical recycling processes involve a lot of mechanical breaking, there is a lot of wear and tear of the machinery. Hence your supersized machine will actually wear out before it even receives the feed load that it is designed for. Also, larger the machine, larger is your electrical consumption. So your per kg cost will go up if you are underutilizing the larger machine. You can always buy a smaller machine and upgrade it. That way you save your capital investment, interest or opportunity cost, keep your operating cost low. When you buy, ensure that the supplier can give you an easy upgrade path for at least a 50% capacity expansion with minimal additional expense.

The typical cost of machinery for this setup can be about 20-25 Lakh INR for supporting a capacity of about 500-750 TPA.

Business Model 3: Level 2 (L2) process, advanced

L2 advanced process is simply about adding a couple of furnaces and the related instrumentation. From a process perspective, everything remains the same. The output, instead of metal fines will now be in the form of ingots. The advantages of this are

    a. Ease of storage and transportation
    b. Ease of inventory management
    c. Better control over theft and pilferage
    d. Better cost realization

e. A larger addressable market for sale
f. Ease of extending operations beyond e-scrap

However, this will add about INR 5 Lakhs to the cost.

Ideally, you should consider this if your collection is beyond 1000 tons per annum. For a smaller collection, the cost per unit of output will become much higher and erode your profits.

Business Model 4: L3 process (semi-automated) with indirect collection

Generally, I do not personally recommend this model for capacities lesser than 3000 tons per annum. This business model is based on an indirect collection method. Hence one can afford to be choosy about the type of scrap to be purchased. In this case, the company buys selected types of e-waste directly from scrap dealers. These suppliers would usually be from the informal space since they are more likely to not have any machinery required for recovering embedded metal. You can also consider imports of specific parts as a source of scrap purchase.

The high level dismantling part gets eliminated in this model. Also, some of the sub-processes such as wire stripping, baling may get eliminated. Procurement of raw material becomes easier.

However, the disadvantages are :

a. A higher cost of raw material
b. Dependency on unreliable suppliers

c. High pilferage of valuable content at suppliers end
d. Increased supplier power can skew the profit equation out of the recycler's favour

So in this model, I suggest that you should be very selective while buying. After all, this is the biggest freedom that this model provides you. You should focus on buying only the scrap that contains precious metals. Since the collections are huge, you need to get into mechanical/automated component level dismantling and assortment. Manual work will increase your cost because you will need so many more people. Besides, the more the labour you employ, your labour management costs, headaches, compliances etc all start eating into your mindshare and wallet-share. You should only process carefully selected components for metal recovery. In this model of semi-automated processing, the metal recovery is largely through manual interventions. It is based on complex metallurgical processes. So you will need people with a decent knowledge of hydrometallurgy and electrometallurgy.

The cost involved in setting up this model is about INR 2-2.5 Crore. Setup time will be quite high. Learning curves will be about a year long. The project will be heavily people dependent. But all this is not really too much to ask for a project that has the potential of earning an ROI of more than 40%.

Business Model 5: Level 3 (L3) advanced

This model is the complete recycling model where you do all collection directly from the waste generation points. You can engage any or all of the methods that you listed at the end of the last chapter. I will strongly recommend this model if your aim is to establish a large setup with a minimum capacity of 5000 tons per annum.

This model is largely automated and needs complex machinery. It includes fully mechanised dismantling and manual sorting over a conveyor. The collection is directly fed to a Pre crusher for size reduction for automated preprocessing. The collected WEEE is broken down into components and isolated through physical inspection over a conveyor belt in order to create batches for efficient further processing. The isolated PCBs are pulverised and the metal and non-metal are separated. All metals are mixed in the output. This mixed metal fraction is then fed into the stage 2 plant. The Stage 2 plant is a separate pyrometallurgical or hydrometallurgical or a hybrid plant. This plant helps in recovering individual precious metals. The finally recovered metals are Copper, Aluminium, Silver, Gold, Palladium etc. The output is in the form of ingots if different metals.

Typically this setup will cost upwards of Rs 25 Crore. Also, the operating costs will be very high, almost about 10-15 Cr annually. However, since the output is a high-value product, it could be a very lucrative option for whoever is willing to invest and be patient for about 3-4 years before the venture breaks even. Beyond that, the project starts delivering an unbelievable ROI of more than 60%, to say the least.

These are the 5 possible business models, each built based on the earlier one as a logical extension to the earlier model. Most people generally prefer to start with model 2 or 3 and then gradually upgrade to model 4. Very few people are interested in directly investing a large amount of money in model 5, especially when they do not have an established collection model.

In fact, it is not even necessary to follow these business models. You can always be ingenious and tweak these basic models to suit your own special interests. There are many recyclers who work in specific niches. For example, some recyclers focus only on refrigerators and Air conditioners for collection, refurbishing as well as recycling. At the same time, there is another breed who is focused purely on resale and refurbishing of IT equipment. I have also met some people focused purely on the telecom sector. And there are yet others who collect everything but are very clearly focused on metal recovery. They are completely disinterested in resale and refurbishing. So ultimately it depends on what you can do and what resonates with you.

Action Time

As an aspiring entrepreneur, you should first estimate your market size, decide on your collection methods and based on the projected collection you can think of the business model suitable for you.

Look at the exercises done in the previous chapters. Especially estimate how much you can collect and decide how much you want to invest in machinery. Use your

SWOT analysis results and the collection techniques that you find most suited to you.

This should help you to identify a business model most suited to you. Decide on your collection targets year on year for the next 5 years and chalk out a plan of how you will like to scale up the business activities and how it can potentially impact your finances. (We have a separate section on finance later. So don't get in the details at this stage. Just limit yourself to your investment and ROI expectations for 5 years.)

Chapter 7

Operations, Processes, and Shopfloor layout

By now you would have realized that a recycling business is quite complex. So just like we have manufacturing processes, standard operating procedures, critical paths, etc in all manufacturing setups, we also have the same complexities in a fairly large recycling setup. Of course, if you are a small entity of anything less than 300 tons per annum, you don't really need to follow any strict processes or apply any operations management concepts. However, irrespective of how small you are if you have the vision and the ambition to grow big, it will make a lot of sense to establish all these practices while you are a small operation.

It is always easier to teach and mould a small child rather than adults!

As mentioned earlier, the plant operations are organized as Level 1 (L1), Level 2 (L2) and Level 3 (L3) processes.

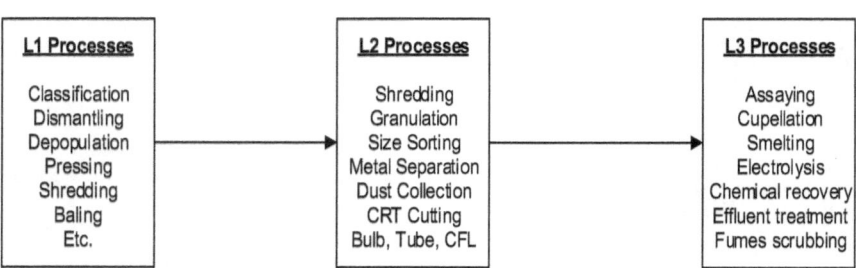

Figure 3: Processing Levels for e-Waste

Obviously, since the processes in each level are different, the requirements of each level of operations are different. You need a different operating flow, a different way of designing your shopfloor, different safety requirements, different ratios of people to machines and so on.

Besides, just like you have these 3 levels of operations inside the plant, you also have some out of plant operations. You also have the flexibility of decentralizing these 3 levels of operations and create a hub and spoke model. Let us look into each of these in a little more details.

Out of Plant Operations

Collection and Transportation Function

Collection and Transportation is a non-process element. However, given the nature of the recycling business, it is the most important component that can make or break it. A strong and reliable collection chain is the biggest competitive advantage that a recycling company can muster. It has the potential of giving a distinctive edge over all other competition. Therefore Collection and Transportation must be made as secure, accountable and efficient as possible. You can use leading-edge technologies such a GPS enabled trucks, route optimization algorithms, supply chain management software etc for building your supply chain. Of course the more you invest, the more is your collection and the bigger you grow.

You can also create an infrastructure wherein you can establish multiple small neighbourhood collection centres within a 5 km-10km radius in each city depending on the population density, traffic conditions, etc. Thus with about 6-8 such centres, the collection coverage can extend up to about 500 sq km. This will ensure local coverage of a large city and its outskirts.

These collection centres can be active centres or simple aggregation points. If your operations are large enough, it makes sense to sue these collection centres also for useful activities such as segregation of working and non-working WEEE.

Of these centres, one can be the main recycling centre or a separate facility may be established for this purpose. That decision will need to be governed based on the availability and suitability of the required land.

It is definitely not mandatory to have such collection centres, but it may encourage people to come and give their e-Waste across the counter. Also, these centres serve as your branding and marketing faces. And very important, if you are interested in the resale and refurbishing business, these centres can also serve as sales outlets for second-hand goods.

I generally suggest outsourcing transport while you are a small operation and later invest in your own transport and logistics infrastructure.

Logistics and Warehousing Function

This will completely depend on the scale of operations. You can also have a multi-city presence, create the above-mentioned infrastructure either yourself or through a franchise network and have a regional warehouse at a city level. This warehouse acts as an aggregation point for your multiple collection centres and temporary warehousing before shipping out to the central processing facility. Besides passive warehousing, you can use this facility for refurbishing or of easily repairable equipment. You can also do an elementary level of Dismantling of non-re-saleable large format equipment. The warehouse can also double up as a used equipment retail store as well as a collection centre depending on its location and other viability parameters.

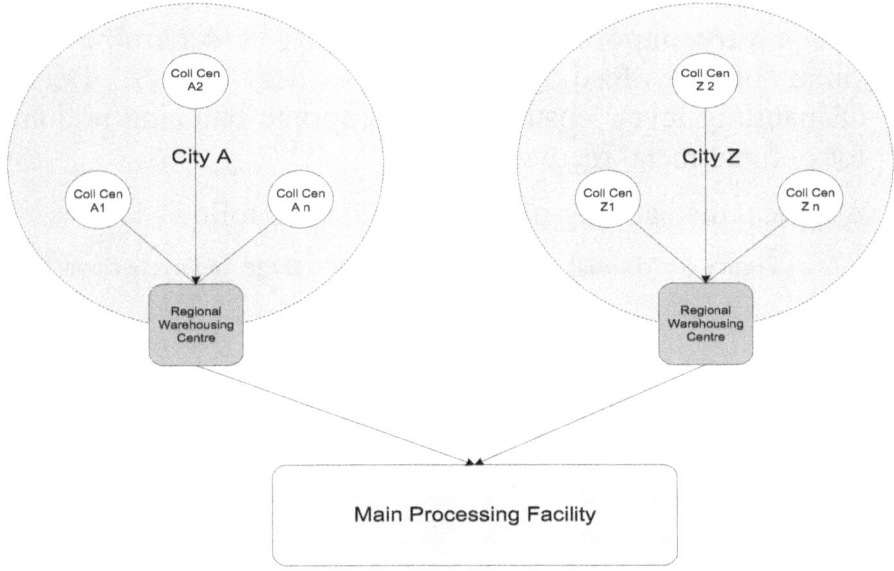

Figure 4: Hub and Spoke Arrangement for e-Waste Collection

Dismantling and Classification Function

While you may do preprocessing for large format electronic equipment at the regional warehouse level to save transportation cost, your warehouse is not a fully equipped dismantling setup. Hence you may dismantle the rest of the equipment at the plant level. Also, your collection will be more and more related to computing and telecom equipment, from a labour perspective it becomes economical to centralize the preprocessing function. This is also a very important function because it determines the value of the feed going in the next stages. Better dismantling levels ensure that appropriate batching is done for optimal metal recovery.

A typical dismantling process will look as follows :

Figure 5 : Manual dismantling : sample stage and cycle times

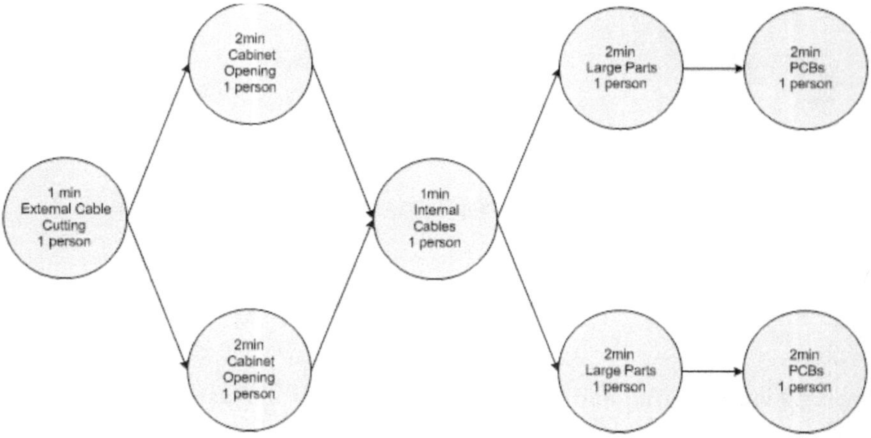

You can design your dismantling process duly supported with the right infrastructure including well-designed tables and equipment. This will bring in a certain discipline and maintain minimum losses at the highest efficiency. Typically you should try to device the flow in such a way that you can achieve a dismantling rate of about 1 or two minutes per equipment. The length of the chain will depend on the nature of the equipment. Be careful not to make the chain too long for achieving this because then it will increase your labour costs. Based on my experience a 4 to 8 link chain is usually good for almost 70-80% of the collection. You can start with 4 nodes and later as you expand or feel the need you can expand or multiply the chains.

Beyond the manual dismantling, the second level of dismantling is at the board level where the mounted components are depopulated from the baseboards. You may want to do this activity at the central processing plant for reasons of cost-saving and reducing pilferage possibilities.

In this PCB depopulation function, all components from the PCB are depopulated and the individual components and the solder are recovered. You will need to classify components as per their intrinsic value. Solder separation at an early stage also helps in precious metal recovery at later stages. Besides, depopulated boards are easier to process and the outputs of both this as well as other downstream processes have higher purity.

You will need to define certain rules for classification suited to your style of working and scope and focus of your activity. For example, you may decide to classify based on a classification tree-like WEEE – Working / Repairable / Scrap

WEEE-Working – IT / Telecom / consumer durables

WEEE-Working – IT – Laptops / Desktops / Printers / Display Screens etc

WEEE-Working – IT – Laptops – High Configuration / Average Configuration / Low configuration

In this fashion, you can develop the classification tree for each type. Ultimately, the aim should be to sell easily, have a reasonable clarity of your salable inventory at any point. Such clarity will help you to create special marketing programs, schemes and offers for offloading your goods and keep your cash flow healthy. Such clear classification will also help you to schedule your dismantling runs and L2 process batches effectively.

This classification and appropriate tagging should be done right at the collection centre based on a predefined SOP.

A manual process is desirable for the purpose of cost optimization as well as judicious interventions for process and profit optimization. Mechanised dismantling is possible, however quite expensive. In case of a completely centralized model and a significantly large comingled collection (> 5000 tons), mechanized dismantling can be used. It is completely your strategic decision of investment in capital versus labour.

Other Sub Processes

But that's not all. On the sidelines of dismantling, there are other processes such as size reduction and baling. These processes are optional. They actually do not add any value to the salable material. However, there is a benefit of ease of maintaining inventory and transportation. You may be compelled to undertake these activities if you have space limitations and / or large collections. However, as I have said earlier, it is useful to introduce discipline just for the sake of it. It pays off in the long run.

Baling / Sheet Pressing

Baling or sheet pressing may be required for efficient storage and transportation of metal and plastic cabinets. Shredding may be essential before baling depending on the material type. You can use a hydraulic or electrically powered baler. Additional Shredder may be used if required before baling. A simple Sheet press can also be used for parts that can be simply pressed into sheets instead of shredding. If you are planning a decentralized model, it may be useful to do this at least at the regional warehouses.

Till this stage, the processes are typically called the Level 1 (L1) stage of recycling. Some types of equipment do not really have L1 and L2 stages. Usually, these are single-stage processes and usually, they are used for negative value items i.e. the cost of running any process on such items is higher than the realizable value of the output after the process.

CRT Recycling

CRT recycling is a negative value business. It essentially comprises of a separate dismantling line where the CRTs are opened, the Tube is cut from the screen, the phosphor coating is removed and separated. The end output is a large amount of plastic, glass, some ferrous metals and copper. Only the copper has a good value. Rest of the by-products do not fetch anything and in fact, you may need to incur some cost to dispose of them. Since CRTs are already near extinction, you may decide not to invest in this and instead have a tie-up with another recycler who has already invested in the infrastructure for CRTs.

CRT cutters are available in both the manual model and an automated model. Manual models use a heating element or a diamond-tipped cutting tool. These need to be manually used for dismantling the CRTs. In the automated model, a laser or an infrared beam do the cutting job. Needless to say, automated CRT cutters are quite expensive as compared to manual ones.

You may have realized that this is not really CRT 'recycling'. There is very little that you recover. It is more of CRT destruction or disposal if you need a gentler word

Refrigerator and AC Recycling

Refrigerators and ACs require a little different setup. Just like any other equipment, it also needs a manual dismantling followed by a series of processes. The key processes are those which involve removal of CFC, separation of coolant and cutting of the compressor. The end output is a large number of active electronics, copper, ferrous metals and good quality of plastics. The separated coolants have to be treated and disposed of. This is not really a negative value item. Just that the equipment has a much larger volume and needs a different type of handling. The revenue realization comes mainly through copper, aluminium and the control circuits.

European technologies are available for this activity. However, I generally recommend a standard manual machine assisted process followed by a separation of metals from the Composite PCBs. You can integrate the required manual processes within the recycling facility with appropriate machinery and pollution control equipment. Alternatively, it may make sense to dispose of refrigerators and air conditioners to recyclers who already have such facilities instead of investing in the same. There are enough recyclers who have an extra capacity within their setup.

Bulbs, Tubes and CFLs

These are another type of negative value material. Some of the bulbs and tubes contain hazardous mercury vapours or sodium vapours. Most of them usually have an inert gas like Neon or Argon. Luckily the presence of mercury is minuscule to trouble us as long as it is a few tubes/bulbs. In recycling facilities where the quantities received are large, it can pose a health hazard. Simple affordable machinery is available for this activity. The end output is a large amount of glass, small amounts of aluminium and copper.

Affordable small machines are available that can handle about 100 tubes per hour. This technology helps in breaking the bulbs and tubes in an enclosed environment and removing the mercury and sulphur vapours through suction. These separated gases are then passed through scrubbers and then let out in the atmosphere. Traces of mercury are trapped in the filters which are later given to landfilling. Large capacity machines are available from European manufacturers that can also help in extracting mercury. However, in the Indian context, it doesn't remain viable.

In-Plant Operations

Once the WEEE is dismantled, the rest of the L2 process is almost completely mechanised. It is important to decide on the capacity of this L2 plant little carefully. If your collection target is, let us say, 1000 Tons per annum, and if you are collecting mixed WEEE without any cherry-picking, on an average you will get about 20% i.e 200 tons of resalable material. Assuming that you do not engage in any repairs and refurbishment and take the rest for recycling, you just have 800 tons. Form this, you need the L2 plant for PCB recycling. PCBs are, on an average, about 25% of the collection. i.e you will have about 200 tons per annum of PCBs for recycling. If you consider 250 working days, you need a processing capacity of about 0.8 tons per day. If you are working in a single shift of 8 hours, it means a processing capacity of just about 100 kg per hour. You can easily scale up the operations to twice this size with the same machinery just by working two shifts. And even a little more by working for 300 days instead of 250 or even more by working 365 days, 24 hours like a typical manufacturing setup. Of course, your machinery should be able to support such a demanding operation. And obviously, it will add to your cost. You can also decide to work with a vendor who can give you an easy and cost-effective capacity expansion plan.

The general process flow of an L2 plant is as under :

Separated components are selectively processed in separate batches.

The bare PCBs after depopulation are fed into a shredder for size reduction through an input conveyor. The shredded fractions are conveyed to a pulverizer. During this transit, the shredded fractions pass under a magnetic separator for separation of ferrous material.

The non-ferrous component is pulverised and the crush is moved pneumatically into a cyclone separator where the dust and material are separated.

The dust is collected in the dust collectors and packed for safe disposal into the CHWSTDF.

The metals are separated from the non-metals using technologies such as density separation or electrostatic separation. The output metal from the bare PCB board is copper and epoxy powder.

If you have a larger facility where you have a fully automated plant, the depopulation is ruled out and the PCBs are directly shredded along with the components. The entire plant assembly takes care of the individual metal separation.

Depopulation Function

This function is already described above in the Out of Plant Operations in case of decentralized operations. Obviously, for a centralized operation, it becomes an in-plant function.

Components from the circuit boards are separated from the baseboard using dry thermal (non-incinerating) process. While there is a possibility of using a chemical process, it can become cumbersome, clumsy and messy to introduce chemicals at this stage. Also, it can result in losses of certain metals like Tin. However, I must say that chemical depopulation is the cheapest method.

Size Reduction Function

Size reduction is required for multiple purposes. Composite material needs to be reduced to powder form to be able to separate the metals trapped between layers of non-metals. It may also be required for efficient warehousing of space-consuming items such as cabinets.

Size reduction is also required for component level processing for precious metal recovery.

Usually, the size reduction process is multi-stage with a shredder or pre crusher for primary size reduction and either a hammer mill or a ball mill for fine crushing. Depending on the material to be crushed, either of the mills may be used.

Metal separation function

Metal from the PCBs can be separated after the fine crushing of the PCB. I generally recommend a density-based metal – non-metal separator. Other technologies such as eddy currents or electrostatic separation are a bit expensive. However, depending on the material in question, they can also be used. In fact, in larger setups, all the 3 methods will tend to co-exist.

Metallurgical Processes

The metal extraction technology is based on hydrometallurgy with supporting electrometallurgical and Pyrometallurgical processes. Hydrometallurgical process has a low operating cost, high recovery rates, and low equipment cost. Equipment required comprise of pipes, valves and reaction tanks fitted with appropriate sensors and controls. Material handling is largely manual. As required, mechanical handling is also done, especially in cases of larger loads and hazardous environments.

Some of the metals are best extracted through pyrometallurgical processes. These processes are necessary for melting and homogenization of metals or complete drying of hygroscopic salts. You may need a couple of furnaces suited for the specific metal and the purpose.

Some of the metals are recovered through an electrolytic process through electrowinning techniques. Electrometallurgical processes may also be required for refining of isolated metals. Generally, it is used for copper and sometimes silver and gold. You will need electrolytic tanks, fluid handling pumps and valves, rectifier, anode making mechanism and some other accessories for the electrolytic tank. Some of the furnaces can be used for anode making.

This method is popular if you are using fully populated PCBs. The metal mixture converted into an ingot and copper is recovered at the cathode. The remaining anodic sludge is further processed for precious metal recovery.

There are many methods including aqua regia method or acid-peroxide method or a halide method or a cyanide method. Aqua regia and cyanide methods are the most commonly used. I generally recommend the aqua regia method is recommended. This relatively slower method as compared to cyanide. However, considering worker safety and relative ease of availability of aqua regia it makes life easier. The gold dissolved in aqua regia is precipitated by cementation in the cementation tank.

Figure 6: Electrowinning Schematic Diagram

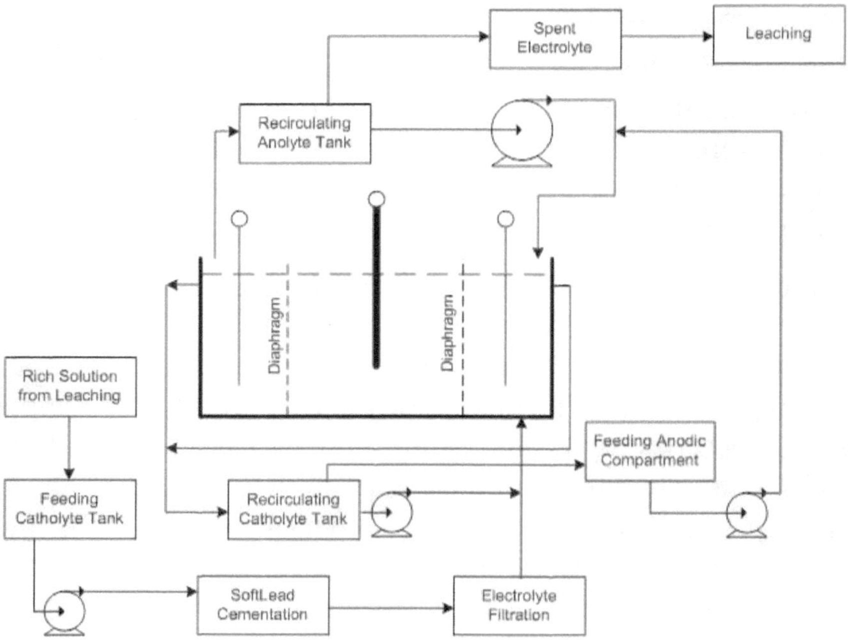

Silver from the remaining silver chloride can be recovered through electrowinning.

Palladium is found in specific components which can be separated at the depopulation stage and treated separately by hydrometallurgical methods. This is a largely manual process considering the small volumes processed.

All of the metals before recovery are also available in form of dissolved salts. These salts can be crystallized and also be directly sold. For example, Silver Chloride and Copper Sulphate have a heavy demand in many industries. Completely crystallized and dry copper sulphate attracts a premium over copper. However by nature, the salt is highly hygroscopic and hence the investment required for the right quality of crystallization, drying, storage and transportation is much higher.

Bio-leaching methods also exist and are best from an environmental perspective. However, the recovery efficiency of the bio-leaching process is very low and hence not preferred by recyclers.

Single Central Processing Plant versus Distributed facility

While for the purpose of this document, these processes are assumed to be executed in a single facility, it is also possible to run them in different facilities. There are pros and cons of both approaches

Advantages of Single Central Processing Pant

1. Better and easier security
2. Lower manpower due to multi-tasking possibility
3. Overall lower investment

Advantages of Distributed Facility

1. Lower transportation cost if the collection is across a larger geography.
2. Easier scalability of operations

Irrespective of the adopted structure, the technology and the overall processes remain more or less the same. After the manual and mechanical dismantling stage, most parts having a single metal/non-metal are separated. These parts are directly baled / sheet pressed and sold to willing buyers such as smelters, pellet makers, etc. Composite parts such as circuit boards and wires need to be processed further to recover metals from them.

At this stage, you may also start wondering about some other types of electronic components that we have not mentioned so far like batteries and LCD panels. Dry cell battery recycling is again based on pulverising and metal separation through chemical processes. However, it is important to completely discharge the batteries before they can be processed, failing which there is a very high explosion potential. Metals such as nickel, cobalt, magnesium and cadmium can be recovered from batteries strictly through a chemical process.

LCD/Plasma/TFT/LED display panels recycling is still under development as of the beginning of 2020. The most sought after metal in these panels is usually indium. However going further, even these display panels are likely to give way to completely virtual displays as we see in many movies. A very coarse version already exists in the form of laser-based imaging.

Having had an overview of these many operating processes, you may now be wondering about how an ideal factory setup should be. Of course, it is completely dependent on how much land you have to construct your facility. Obviously, the scale and scope of operations will also determine the final layout. Essential considerations that you need to keep in mind are safety factors and emergency exits. Ventilation and natural light are important considerations. From an operational perspective, you need to design your material flows and keep enough space for material and people movement without creating any bottlenecks. A good industrial architect can guide you well.

You will need to know and list down all the equipment that you will need so that you can decide the machinery locations. Also, you may need to know the equipment sizes. Most vendors will give you a GA drawing and a tentative floor plan for their equipment. Of course, you cannot get everything through a single vendor. So, let us make a list of all the possible equipment that we may need for a decently sized e-waste setup (say 1000-2000 TPA capacity recycling facility)

List of Equipment / Tools

Based on the above discussion, the following list of equipment was drawn. Please note that this list of equipment is for a single central plant. Depending on the organizational architecture chosen, and the capacities at each of the organizational elements, the quantities of the equipment will change.

1. Weighbridge and weighing machines
2. Overhead crane for material movement
3. Dismantling Line
4. Pallete trucks, forklifts
5. Hydraulic stacker
6. Bins, crates, trolleys
7. Dismantling line
8. Dust collection for dismantling line
9. Depopulation machine
10. Fune scrubber for depopulation machine
11. Sorting conveyors
12. Shredder (For PCBs)
13. Pulveriser with cyclone separator
14. Ball mill
15. Intermediate Conveyors
16. Magnetic Separators
17. Dust Collector for crushing mills
18. Sheet Press
19. Baler (Hydraulic)
20. Leaching Tanks
21. Pipelining and flow control valves
22. Induction furnace with ingot trays and rails
23. Electrolytic tank
24. Smelting and anodizing system
25. Gas scrubber
26. ETP for hydrometallurgical processes

Apart from this basic list, there would be many small items that you will need. However, for space planning and factory layout, this list is good enough.

Figure 7: Complete process flow diagram

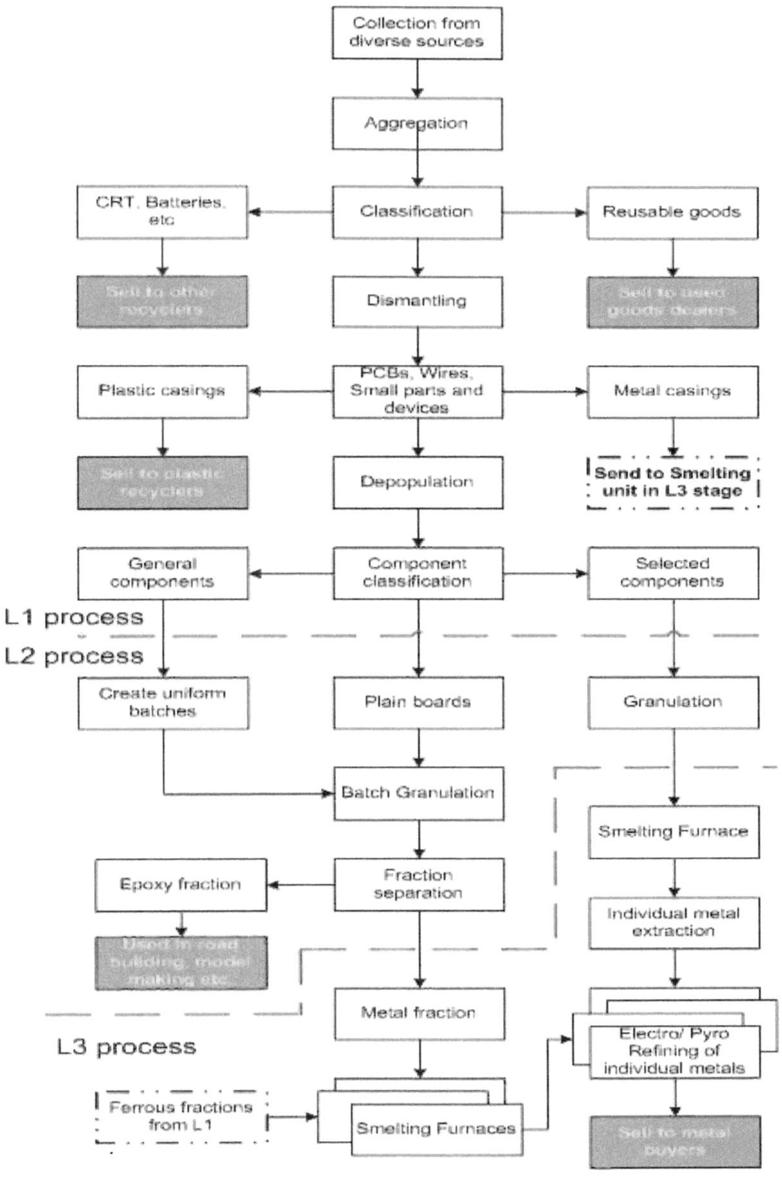

Figure 8: Generic Plant Layout

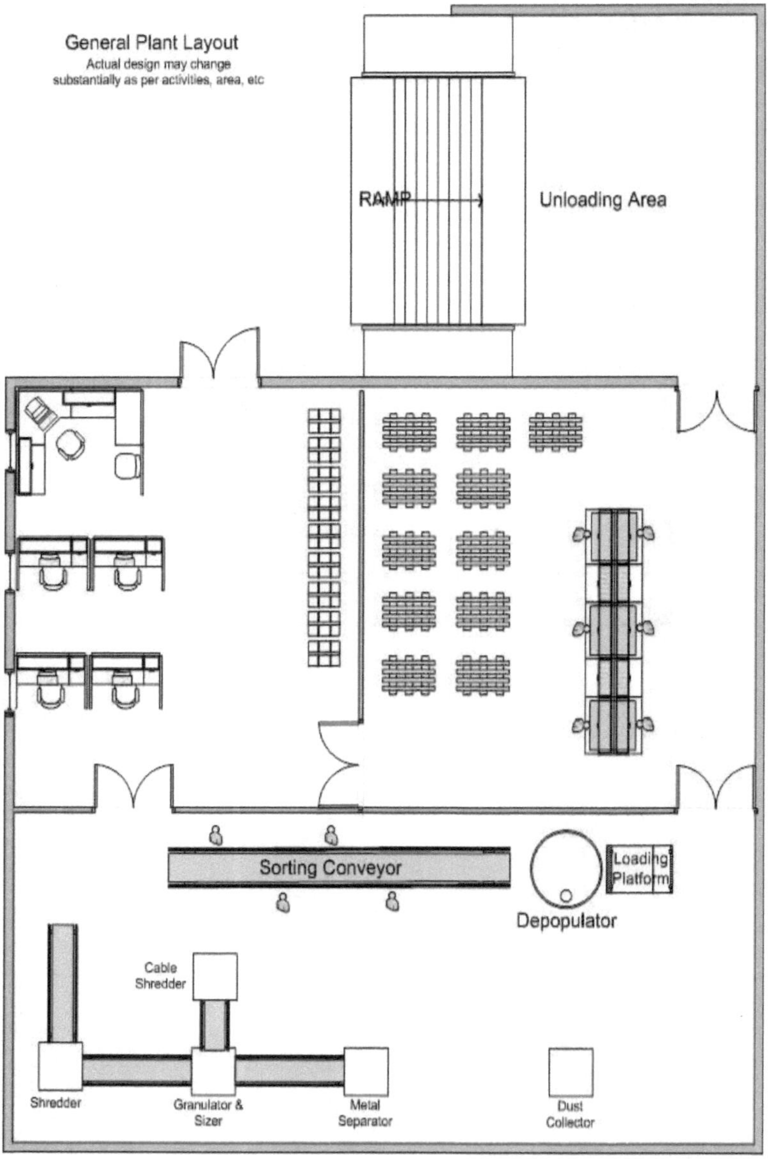

General Plant Layout
Actual design may change
substantially as per activities, area, etc

RAMP

Unloading Area

Sorting Conveyor

Depopulator

Loading Platform

Cable Shredder

Shredder

Granulator & Sizer

Metal Separator

Dust Collector

Action Time

Decide from a practical perspective which of these business models suits you. Do not bother about the investment at this stage. Assuming that you have all the resources at your disposal and considering your own SWOT analysis done earlier, select the model that you are most comfortable with. Based on this model, go through the list of equipment and select what all you will need. You can apply your mind to make this list more exhaustive. Please note that the list given in this chapter is sufficient, but not complete. So go ahead and draw your own list and think about the quantities of each of them.

Chapter 8

Functional Elements: Machinery details and technical comparison

One of the major concerns of an aspiring startup entrepreneur is that he is usually new to the industry and does not really know which all machinery he will need and how should go about evaluating machines and vendors. So, if you are already getting overwhelmed with all the information that you have read so far, relax. We have already listed down all the core equipment. This chapter will help you arrive at a comparison method for most important equipment from that list. For the sake of brevity, we shall look only at the functional elements.

Size Reduction Function

As we have seen earlier, the size reduction function comprises two primary elements i.e the shredder and the pulveriser. Shredders are used to reduce the size of the whole components to smaller pieces. Yet, these small pieces are still small enough for the embedded metal layers to separate from the non-metals. A pulveriser is used to grind the shredded parts into finer powder of less than a few mm in size.

The logic of choice and selection criteria for Shredders: The Shredder types considered are Single shaft, dual shaft and quad shaft shredders. Based on the characteristics of the material, it is clear that a high torque and low-speed rotary shear is required. Though these characteristics are available in all the 3 types, given that we shall be shredding PCBs, the mechanical and electrical efficiency was found the highest in a dual shaft shredder. In case you are considering a very large facility, you may want to consider a large single shaft shredder as your elementary pre crusher followed by some elementary sorting and then again followed by a dual shaft shredder.

Table 6: Comparison of Shredding Technologies

	Single Shaft	Twin Shaft / Dual Shaft	Quad Shaft
Torque	High	High	High
Speed	Low	Low	Low
Throughput	Low	High	High
Consumable cost	High	Low	Low
Shaft weight	High	Low	Low
Power at no Load	High	Low	High
Power at Full Load	High	Medium	High
Motor Size	Large	Small	Small, Multiple
Gear Box	Large	Small	Small, Multiple
Transmission	Geared, direct	Chain-Sprocket/ Belt-Pulley	Chain-Sprocket/Belt-Pulley

The logic of choice and selection criteria for Pulveriser: The pulveriser types are Ball mill, Vertical spindle roller mill, Ring and Ball Mill, Attrition Mill, Beater Wheel Mill and Hammer Mill. For our purpose of pulverising shredded e-waste, the output of a hammer mill and a Ball mill is found to be comparable. The other types of pulverisers do not work very well for us. The essential differences between Ball Mill and Hammer Mill are in terms of working principle, time to process, space requirement, cost of installation power requirement etc. Other criteria such as possibilities of open and closed circuit grinding, cost of grinding medium, possibilities of batch and continuous operation are found to be more or less similar. From a process perspective, you will need to use both at different application stages. For populated or depopulated PCBs, hammer mill performs better. For CPUs and ICs, ball mill performs better.

Table 7: Comparison of Pulverization technologies

	Hammer Mill	Ball Mill
Grinding technology	Hammers and liner	Balls and liner
Hardness of Feed	High Range	High Range
Open Circuit Grinding	Yes	Yes
Closed Circuit Grinding	Yes	Yes
Batch Process	Yes, Small batch sizes	Yes, Large Batch Sizes
Continuous Process	Yes	Yes
Installation Cost	High	Low
Power requirement	High	Low
Noise generation	High frequency	Low frequency

Metal separation technology

The mechanical metal separation technology choices are between Aspiration and fluidized vibrating bed. The selection is largely dependent on the pulverising method used. In case of the hammer mill, a density-based separation on a fluidized bed is required. In case of a Ball Mill, since the epoxy material of the circuit board was crushed into fine powder by the impact of the rolling balls, aspiration system is more desirable. However considering that the output of the ball mills will be of a low volume and will directly go in the L3 plants, separation is not mandatory, though advisable.

In an aspiration unit, controlled air suction pressure provides aspiration and separates the metal particles based on density difference. An air blower and a battery of cyclones along with a dust collector form the complete assembly of the metal separation unit.

In case of a fluidized bed, you have water and air-based options. Water-based separation is generally preferred in case of ores. For e-waste also, water-based machinery can be used. However, you will need to add a drying process after the separation. Wet metals will generally tend to corrode faster. I generally prefer air as the floatation agent. The crush spread over the fluidized bed, inclined at a specific degree and vibrated at a precalibrated frequency separates by virtue of a combination of mechanical forces.

Eddy currents and Electrostatic separators are also other methods that can be used. Eddy current is a very expensive method and usually suited for applications where individual pieces for separation are more than 4-5 inch in size. If you have a large setup with a huge single shaft pre crusher that would break all equipment directly without any dismantling, adding an eddy current separation system after the shredder will be useful.

Electrostatic separators are a very good option for fluidized bed separation. However, it is expensive.

The separated metals are then subjected to metallurgical processes as discussed in the earlier section.

Table 8: Comparison of dry mechanical metal separation technologies

	Cyclone Separation / Aspiration	Fluidized Bed Separation
Complexity	High	High
Cost	Low	High
Power Consumption	Low	High
Efficiency	Medium	High
Deciding factor	Density	Specific Gravity
Throughput	High	High
Granule size restriction	Nil	Nil
Concept	Pneumatic	Mechanical
Maintenance	Low	High

Metallurgical Processes

There are different metallurgical processes and depending on the properties of each metal, a specific metallurgical technique is most suited for it. It also depends on the physical form of the material from which the metal is to be recovered. Generally, in the case of e-waste processing and metal recovery, pyrometallurgical, hydrometallurgical and electrometallurgical processes will need to co-exist. All the processes have their own pros and cons. Considering the variety of metals included in e-waste, no single process is found suitable for all the metals. Also, considering the concentration of metals, it is found that all of them may not even be recoverable or worth recovering.

Copper Recovery

Copper recovery Is best done through electrowinning when copper is mixed with other elements. In the process that we have discussed so far, the majority of the copper is recovered at the L2 stage itself from the PCBs using mechanical separation. This copper is not refined and does contain some impurities. Most of these non-metallic impurities are burnt in a furnace when you convert the copper into ingots. Depending on the end-use, you can also add certain other metals such as zinc or nickel or any other for rendering the desired properties to Copper.

However, in case you desire a higher purity of copper you may decide to use your electrolysis tanks. The first step is to make anodes from the metal crush by smelting in a furnace and burning out non-metallic impurities. Copper is recovered from these anodes through electrowinning. The remaining anodic sludge goes further for metallurgical processes.

Also, at L3 levels, in the hydrometallurgical processes, copper sulphate, nitrate or chloride may be produced depending on the mother reaction. These salts are produced in aqueous form. Copper can be extracted from these salts through electrolysis.

Silver Recovery

Silver is usually obtained in the form of Silver nitrate or Silver chloride as a by-product of the chemical processes used for gold and other precious metals recovery. Electrolysis is the most suitable method for recovering silver from its salts. The recovered silver is melted in a furnace and converted into ingots.

Gold Recovery :

Gold recovery is done mostly from the anodic sludge obtained in the electrowinning of copper and from the crush of certain components. This raw material typically has a mixture of Gold, silver, platinum and palladium. The quantities available for processing are usually low and a 5 kg plant is good enough for processing. (This size depends on the total collection and its quality). Within the PGM metal recovery plant, the competing methods are cyanide leaching and aqua regia leaching. While cyanide is faster and more effective, usually it is banned in many places due to its highly hazardous nature. Aqua Regia methods are usually used. The system comprises of a series of mixing and settling tanks fitted with valves and pumps as required. Filtration occurs at many places and filtrates and sludge are treated separately as per their nature. This system requires human monitoring and interventions from time to time.

Usually, precious metal recovery vendors will not discuss their recovery processes very easily. It is important that you should ask them deep probing questions. Many times, vendors may be talking about precious metals recovery and refining based on their experience in the jewellery recycling space. I strongly suggest that you must run a proof of concept demonstration before you even get into a price discussion. Recovering precious metals from e-waste a completely different ball game as compared to doing so from scrapped jewellery. In the case of jewellery, the gold contains a small amount of impurity. In the case of e-waste, gold itself is a small amount of impurity within the base metals! Obviously, the equations change significantly.

Evaluation of Vendors

Understanding and evaluating technology is relatively easy. Despite that, I generally suggest that you should hire a consultant to do so. It is every bit worth the money. Generally in a similar product comparison, if you do a spreadsheet comparison, good competitors tend to get a tick against each parameter. The differences are usually very subtle. A consultant can do that job for you.

Vendor evaluation is the trickier part. You will most likely never see a vendor who would openly tell you his weaknesses. You will need to probe and find out. Only a brutally honest vendor will be transparent. (Not that anyone is dishonest, but the brutality of honesty may differ!). So ask the vendor to show you a demonstration to start with. Generally, if they can show you a demonstration of their machinery without putting in too many hurdles, you can say they are confident about their products. Many vendors may say that they can show you a machine functional in a country 3000 miles away. That hardly makes any sense. At the same time, be aware that arranging for a demo at their customer's location is not always easy for any vendor. There are many considerations including the customer's inconvenience.

You may ask them their customer list for a reference check. Usually, that should not be a problem unless they have some kind of non-disclosure agreement with their customers.

You can ask about their support plan. How can they support you? What level is training will they provide you? How will the spares be made available? What is their response times? What is the standard method of raising a trouble ticket? Do they have a dedicated support team available locally? Not that the vendors will have positive answers to all of these. However, the way they answer these questions should give you an insight into what you are getting into.

Be sure to ask about the cost of consumables as well as the delivery times.

And if you are importing machinery, be sure that you know all the necessary documentation and procedures even before you place the order. If for any reason your shipment clearance takes longer time, the customs will charge you a demurrage fee which is way too expensive. Also, you can ask your vendor about whether he can give you a price for delivery at your doorstep with all duties, clearances, insurance, freight etc. all paid up. If you are importing, insist on a quote with incoterms specified.

All said and done, ultimately the vendor's intent matters. Probe into the vendor's mission and vision statements. Find out for yourself through indirect questions about their value systems. How does the vendor see himself? A machine manufacturer? A Solution provider? A business partner? An environmental change-maker? And you may do well to check this out with multiple people within the vendor's team. The consistency of their answers will help you to understand them better.

Remember, price and product features will cease to be significant the moment you make the advance payment. What will matter for the rest of the time in the lifetime of your machine will be the vendor's attitude. Especially when you are a startup business, your vendor can be your biggest asset.

Action Time

In the last chapter, you have already made a list of all the key equipment that matter for production depending on your business model.

For each of the equipment, make a list of your top 3-5 vendors. More vendors will only eat into your time and there may not be any significant incremental benefit.

Make a comparison matrix comprising of various parameters such as product specifications, price, vendor's focus, product range, support policy, spares availability, installation, commissioning and training support, payment terms, ability and willingness to go out of the way to help you, and so on.

For each of these parameters, assign the importance for each of them in terms of %age. The total of all should add up to 100.

Against each parameter give your vendor a score that you feel is right. You can score on a scale of 1 to 5 or 1 to 10, 1 being the lowest in desirability.

Multiply each score by the weight i.e the %age importance assigned to that parameter. Add all the results for each vendor. The comparison of each vendor's total weighted score will give you a mathematical indication of the best-suited vendor.

You can use the below template

Evaluation Parameter	Weightage	Vendor A	
		Score	Weighted Score
Price	30%		
Payment terms	5%		
Taxes / Custom Duty	2%		
Total transport cost	5%		
Warranty period	1%		
Installation and commissioning fees	2%		
User Training	2%		

Maintenance Training	5%		
Service charges during warranty	3%		
Post-warranty support policy	5%		
Cost of spares	10%		
Main business line	5%		
Vendor flexibility for providing support	5%		
Assistance in collection	10%		
Any other types of support	10%		
Total Weighted score	100%		

You may add some more parameters such as support in business operations, sales and marketing advisory, valuation advisory, etc. The weights mentioned herewith are for example only. You may change the weights as per your understanding. Just ensure that the total of the weight is 100%.

Multiply each score by the weight to get the weighted score. Add up the weighted scores.

Of course, this is a mathematical model. You may go beyond this and decide based on your gut feeling. However, with this tool, you will get a rational basis for your final decision.

Chapter 9

Financial projection and calculation methods

One of the main questions you had in mind ever since you started thinking about e-waste was about the money. Even before you picked up this book, you have been looking forward to this section. Let me caution you at this stage. You are likely to uncover some unbelievable numbers and astronomical profits. But keep in mind that this is ultimately theory. We will try to ensure that the theory is as close to reality as possible. Nevertheless, the reality could be quite different, especially in the beginning few years.

Having said that, let us get on with the most important question. How much money can we make?

Ahem, …let us keep that answer for the last. But let us establish a logical model to arrive at that answer. Because, without that logic in place, if I give you the answer, it may be a little too overwhelming!

So let us start with the basic underlying assumptions. You can list down certain assumptions based on your exercises done in the previous chapters. For the sake of simplicity and ease of understanding, I am using a decent-sized business i.e 1000-2000 TPA recycling business. For this business, I will generally list down some assumptions as under. You can list down yours as well.

1. Capital Structure : 30% equity and 70% debt.

2. Collection: Collection target 1000 Tons in year 1 and a consistent 20 % increase year on year.

3. The e-waste collection would be a mix of IT and Non-IT products as per general observations mentioned earlier in this book.

4. Cost of such scrap is assumed to be Rs 30/- per KG. For working equipment that can be easily resold, the cost is estimated to be Rs 250/- per KG. This assumption is based on currently prevailing prices in the market for commonly available scrap.

5. Transportation is assumed to be using various modes and the cost is averaged across all the modes of transport. Taken at Rs 10 per kg.

6. Insurance costs are not taken into consideration since that will depend on various riders and provisions of insurance that is opted for.

7. Spare inventory for plant maintenance is not considered. However, maintenance cost is considered 10% every year.

8. Land cost is NOT taken into consideration. However, rent is included as a substitute for the opportunity cost of capital if the land is bought outright or previously owned.

9. The building is assumed to cost Rs 50 Lakhs.

10. All operating costs and revenue realization increase by 10 % year on year.

11. Directors' compensation is tied directly to the financial performance of the company and is considered as 10% of the revenue by sales.

You may decide to vary these numbers as per your judgment and/or information.

Capital Expenses

Capital expenses are less of a worry since they are one time. Also, if you consider it in comparison with the operating expenses, they are the minor component. Third, it is much easier to get finance for capital expenditures as compared to operating expenses.

The Capex components are

      a. Factory Building with office furniture, fixtures, workbenches, shopfloor, tech equipment, etc.
      b. Plant and Machinery.

Operational Expenses

Operational expenses are crucial for the long term survival of the business. This will affect your cash flow directly. At the same time, lowering operating expense may also mean lowering the scale of the activity which is certainly not desirable. For a given scale of a business, you will need to incur a specific minimum expense anyways. Generally, in manufacturing setups, the operating expense per unit of production is a key metric to follow. Lower the per-unit cost, the better it is for business. Obviously, it doesn't mean that a lower total opex is desirable.

The Opex components are -

    a. Salaries. (For different models, the staff required is different. You will need to estimate the staff and their salaries based on your local markets.)
    b. Cost of scrap
    c. Utility expenses such as electricity and water.
    d. Logistics expenses
    e. Marketing expenses
    f. Spares and consumables
    g. Contingency expenses

Please note that I am trying to help you arrive at your own projections in this exercise. Hence I will not be giving out a complete projected financial statement, rather I will be outlining the method to arrive at the same. So you are encouraged to open your spreadsheets and use your own numbers. You can use the concepts, ideas and methods given here or you can devise your own as well. Either way, you will be right in the long run if you implement the project with your heart in it!

Common Sample Calculations

Table 9 : Collection Targets

		Year 1	Year 2	Year 3
Collection (Tons)		1000	1200	1440
IT	60%	600	720	864
Non IT	40%	400	480	576

Table 10 : Composition of IT and telecom Waste

		Year 1	Year 2	Year 3
Metal cabinets	50%	300.00	360.00	432.00
Plastic cabinets	10%	60.00	72.00	86.40
Circuit boards	20%	120.00	144.00	172.80
Wires	10%	60.00	72.00	86.40
Batteries and Others	10%	60.00	72.00	86.40

Table 11: Composition of Consumer electronics and other non-IT waste

		Year 1	Year 2	Year 3
Metal	50%	200.00	240.00	288.00
Plastic	20%	80.00	96.00	115.20
Circuit Boards	5%	20.00	24.00	28.80
Wires	15%	60.00	72.00	86.40
Glass and others	10%	40.00	48.00	57.60

Table 12 : Cost of Transportation

Vehicle	Capacity (kg)	Utilization	Avg Wt	Avg trip cost	Coverage	cost/kg
Hand cart	100	50%	50	300	2km	6.0
3 wheeler tempo	250	50%	125	800	10km	6.4
4 wheeler tempo	500	50%	250	3000	20km	12.0
Mid size truck	1000	50%	500	6000	50km	12.0

(4 W)							
Full size truck (6 W)	4000	50%	2000	15000	100km	7.5
Large size truck (16 w)	20000	50%	10000	30000	200 km	3.0
						7.8
					Assume	**10**

Now based on these basic numbers we will need to build the bigger picture. For this picture, I shall be assuming, as mentioned earlier, a decently sized recycling business focused on copper and aluminium recovery. Rest of the precious metal bearing components shall be sold in the markets. (Does this sound like our Business model 2 or 3?)

As I have mentioned earlier, direct collection is key; we shall use this key to unlock our fortunes! We shall go by our business model 2/3 and resale easily resalable goods and recycle everything else.

One of the most important components of operating costs is salary. So we will need to estimate the number of people. One way of doing it is to list down all the tasks that are required to be done. You can refer to chapter 7 for the business processes. Based on that list, identify how many people may be required for each task, whether multitasking is possible, etc. Decide the salary that you will be willing to pay for each person hired. You will get the annual numbers. Please keep in mind that as your collection increases every year, the number of some of the people will increase. You can easily calculate this with a spreadsheet for 5 years or as many as you want. You may either do this exercise on an annual basis or a quarterly basis or a more granular monthly basis. The finer you go, the better you will be in control of your cash flow. However, it could be a tedious exercise to go to anything lower than a quarterly period.

The second most significant part of the operating costs is the scrap procurement cost. Based on your target, you can slice it up into quarterly or monthly. You may also do it annually to get a sense of the big numbers.

Based on the scrap collection, you can now identify the processes and the machinery used for each process. Calculate the machine utilization against its rated capacity. This will help you to arrive at the power expense.

For example, if we consider the depopulation process, your calculation should look like this. Please note that these are sample numbers and not actuals. You will need to calculate them based on all the tips shared in earlier chapters.

Table 13: Machine capacity and utilization calculations

The calculation for depopulator (example)	Y1	Y2	Y3
Approx PCB weight influx per shift of 8 hours (Tons)	0.14	0.17	0.21
Depopulator capacity per hour (Tons)	0.1		
No of hours required	1.43	1.72	2.06

Table 14: Power Consumption

Power cost per unit	10			
List of machines	Power rating			

		in KW			
Depopulation Line	22	9460.00	11352.00	13622.40
Sorting Conveyor	2.4	5760.00	5760.00	5760.00
Total Power cost (lakhs)		**1.52**	**1.88**	**2.35**

Similarly, you will need to list down all processes and arrive at their capacity utilization and

Table 15: Investment schedule

List of machinery	Qty	Approx Unit Price	Y1	Y2	Y3
Classification Bins	50	0.05	2.50		
Hydraulic Stackers (Manual)		0.9	1.80		
Wheel Barrows	4	0.1	0.40		
Depopulation line	1	9	9.00		
8 node Dismantling line	1	2	2.00		
Wire stripper	1	0.75	0.75		
CRT Cutting machine	1	3	3.00		
Total A			**19.45**	**0.00**	**0.00**
Machine Maintenance		10%	1.95	2.14	2.35
Manpower Costs			55.20	60.72	66.79
Scrap Purchase			780.00	1029.60	1359.07
Transportation			90.00	108.00	129.60
Electricity			1.52	1.88	2.35
Water			2.00	2.20	2.42
Land Rent			24.00	26.40	29.04
Total B			954.67	1230.94	1591.62
Building			25		
Total A + B + C			**999.12**	**1230.94**	**1591.62**

Notes :

Prices for machinery are indicative. This is not an official quote.

Scrap purchase cost is based on assumption as explained in the assumptions section.

Transportation is calculated as explained in the earlier text

Electricity cost is calculated as rated expense x utilization

Maintenance cost is assumed to be 10% of the original machine cost and is assumed to increase steadily by 25% year on year from 3rd year onwards.

Table 16 : Capital requirement (lakhs)

Initial Capital	2 month Opex		159.11
Total Starting capital	**2 months Opex + Capex**		**203.56**
Owner's equity		30%	61.07
Loan		70%	142.49

Revenue estimation

In model 2, the business process is extended beyond dismantling and direct selling of components. Instead, we now focus on isolating metals from non-metals and try to segregate as much metal as possible from the collected e-scrap using a completely dry mechanical process. The output is in the form of metal fines/grains.

Table 17: Revenue realization

Revenues from PCB					
Components	Content^S %	Rate (INR/Kg)*	Year 1	Year 2	Year 3
High Value Ics	3%	700	24.15	31.88	42.08

Low Value Ics	5%	300	17.25	22.77	30.06
Copper from Base Boards	20%	300	69.00	91.08	120.23
Capacitors	10%	15	1.73	2.28	3.01
Heat sinks	5%	40	2.30	3.04	4.01
Connectors/ fingers	2%	600	13.80	18.22	24.05
Solder	4%	500	23.00	30.36	40.08
Epoxy and Glass	16%	0	0.00	0.00	0.00
Estimated revenue (A)			**151.23**	**199.62**	**263.49**

Revenues from Wires

Components	Content^S %	Rate (INR/Kg)*	Year 1	Year 2	Year 3
PVC	40%	2	0.84	1.11	1.46
Copper (Cu)(Lme rate 434)	60%	300	189.00	249.48	329.31
Estimated revenue (B)			**189.84**	**250.59**	**330.78**

Revenues from Metal Body

Components	Content^S %	Rate (INR/Kg)*	Year 1	Year 2	Year 3
Iron (Fe) (Lme Rate 25.8)	100%	20	70.80	93.46	123.36
Removable Copper from large parts	100%	300	114.00	150.48	198.63
Estimated revenue (C)			**184.80**	**243.94**	**322.00**

Revenues from Glass and Plastic

Components	Content^S %	Rate (INR/Kg)	Year 1	Year 2	Year 3

Resins and Plastics	25%	10	2.86	3.78	4.98
Glass	75%	0.5	0.43	0.51	0.62
Estimated revenue (D)			**3.29**	**4.29**	**5.60**
Revenue from Resale					
Total Resalable e-Waste			140.00	168.00	201.60
Cost of acquisition (per Kg)	250		350.00	462.00	609.84
Total Cost			476.00	628.32	829.38
Profit from Resale	100%		476.00	628.32	829.38
Estimated revenue (E)			**952.00**	**1256.64**	**1658.76**
Total Revenue (A+B+C+D+E)			**1481.15**	**1955.07**	**2580.63**

Projected Financial Statements

Typically you will need to generate 3 different statements. The projected profit and loss statement will establish whether or not the business will earn any operating profits. The cash flow statement will help you know about your liquidity position and ensure that your profits are real and not notional. This is the most important part of your financial statements because your cashflow will establish the long term sustainability of the project. Finally, you need the projected balance sheet. This will summarize both your company's assets and liabilities and help to establish your company's net worth.

Ideally, you would need a minimum of 5 years projection. Some investors may also ask you to give a 7 or a 10 years projection. It is also useful if you work it out quarterly instead of annually.

Table 18: Sample Projected Profit and Loss statement

	Year 1	Year 2	Year 3
Revenue from Sales	**1481.15**	**1955.07**	**2580.63**
Operating Expenses			
Salaries	54.84	60.32	72.16
Rent	24.00	26.40	29.04
Raw Material	780.00	987.60	1253.23
Utilities	16.01	18.96	22.48
Transportation	90.00	108.00	129.60
Spares and consumables	5.23	5.75	6.32
Directors Compensation	74.06	97.75	129.03
Others and Contingency	148.12	195.51	258.06
Total	**1192.24**	**1500.29**	**1899.94**
PBIDT	**288.91**	**454.78**	**680.70**
Interest Paid (18 % pa)	21.86	18.15	13.89
Depreciation (on p&m @ 15 %, WDV)	7.84	6.66	5.66
Depreciation (on building @ 5 %, WDV)	1.25	1.19	1.13
PBT	**257.96**	**428.78**	**660.01**
Tax @ 30.9 %	64.49	107.20	165.00
PAT	**193.47**	**321.59**	**495.01**
Dividend paid	58.04	96.48	148.50
Tax on dividend @ 17%	9.87	16.40	25.25

Transferred to General Reserves	125.56	208.71	321.26

Table 19: Sample Projected cash flow statement

	Year 1	Year 2	Year 3
Cash Receipts			
Opening Cash Balance	0	1165.74	2407.81
Share Capital	71.68		
Bank loan	167.25		
PBIDT	1192.24	1500.29	1899.94
Total	**1431.17**	**2666.03**	**4307.75**
Cash Payments			
Capex (for plant and machinery)	52.25		
Capex (for Building)	25.00		
Repayment of principal	24.84	28.55	32.81
Interest on loans	21.86	18.15	13.89
Depreciation on machinery (7 yrs, WDV)	7.84	6.66	5.66
Depreciation (on building @ 5 %, WDV)	1.25	1.19	1.13
Taxes @ 30.9%	64.49	107.20	165.00
Dividend	58.04	96.48	148.50
Tax on dividend@17%	9.87	16.40	25.25
Total	**265.44**	**258.22**	**367.00**
Closing Cash Balance	**1165.74**	**2407.81**	**3940.75**

Table 20: Sample Projected balance sheet

	Year 1	Year 2	Year 3
Sources of Funds			
Owner's equity			
Share Capital	71.68	71.68	71.68
Reserves and Surplus	125.56	208.71	321.26
Loan Funds			
Secured loan	142.41	113.86	81.05
Total	**339.65**	**394.25**	**473.99**
Application of Funds			
Fixed assets			
Plant and Machinery	52.25	44.41	37.75
Less Accumulated Depreciation	7.84	6.66	5.66
Building	25.00	23.75	22.56
Less Accumulated Depreciation	1.25	1.19	1.13
Net Block	**68.16**	**60.31**	**53.52**
Current Assets			
Cash (Working Capital + WIP Inventory)	271.49	333.93	420.47
Less Current Liabilities	0.00	0.00	0.00
Total Current Liabilities	0.00	0.00	0.00
Net current Assets	**271.49**	**333.93**	**420.47**
Total Assets	**339.65**	**394.25**	**473.99**

Action Time

This whole chapter is primarily an exercise for working out your project viability. Just use the templates give herein. Plugin your own numbers. The numbers mentioned herein are for model 2 as described earlier in this book. You can reverse calculate the formulae used and create your own spreadsheets for creating different scenarios. You can plug in the numbers that you choose at the critical inputs and see how your equations change.

Please note that the numbers mentioned herein are for example only.

Chapter 10

Risk Analysis and Mitigation Measures

For any business, there are risks. Higher the risks, higher the rewards. However, that does not mean that we should take irrational risks. Higher rewards do come with higher risks provided those risks are all calculated and you have mitigation plans in place. Should something go wrong, you should always trigger your safety nets and activate your response plan.

A business always has both internal and external risks. Internal systemic risks arise from issues internal to the organization such as business process failures, inventory control failures, equipment failures, labour problems etc. Typically these are risks over which you can have control. You can detect these risks well in advance if you have the right triggers in place. For example, if your inventory is not moving you will know it and you can put efforts to liquidate it. Of if your machinery keeps failing often, you may be able to look into your operating processes, your material and can engage your vendor to address this. You will need to have an efficient crisis management person or a team.

Though as mentioned, such internal risks can be addressed as they come, it is always better to mitigate them beforehand. You may decide to get your shopfloor processes designed by professionals. You can get your operating staff properly trained and engage operations experts for setting up standards and best practices. Ideally, the entire process must be certified for standards compliance such as ISO 9001 / 14001. The staff must be trained in following these processes regularly and periodic audits must be conducted both internally and externally to ensure that the processes are up to date and efficient.

For Inventory control failures, technology can be of great assistance. There are certain specific ERPs tuned for waste management. You can also engage a good technology consultant to devise a special software for you. Over and above this inventory management or ERP software you may use real-time or near real-time analytical software to get an excellent handle over inventory and allow for quick what-if scenarios. There are many cloud-based cost-effective analytics products available. You should ideally select an analytics software such that you as a business user must be able to tweak the parameters themselves and not need a high tech person for managing it for you. This is highly necessary because of the inherent communication and vision gap between the top management or business strategy team and the technology team.

The risk of equipment failures is almost non-existent because most of the vendors provide some real good pieces of engineering. However, failures can happen if you have chosen to buy machines in piecemeal from multiple vendors. Capacity mismatches between machines can cause problems. Incorrect utilization of machinery can cause problems. So your operators must be trained properly. Also, you can maintain some onsite stocks or maintenance spares.

You can also engage the equipment manufacturer in a stringent SLA contract. It may cost you a bit but that cost is worth paying rather than production going down. On-site maintenance engineers may be extensively trained by the manufacturer and appropriate periodic preventive maintenance must be carried out. You can have an in-house team of technicians.

Labour risks are a common and most probable event among all the internal risks. Such risk can only be mitigated by an effective HR policy. You can think of some regular incentives based on output, performance-based rewards systems etc. Apart from financial rewards, most people need a good working environment, a forward-looking growth path and appreciation. Your vision and mission statements that you have defined in the beginning are useful here. Each person of your team must believe in the vision and the mission. You will need to make them understand the bigger goal and align your organizational goal with their personal aspirations. That will make them accept the organizational goal as their own goal. If this happens, most labour problems will cease to exist.

External risks are usually out of the company's control and hence nothing much can be done to mitigate such risks. However, some respite may be sought in certain situations through internalizing external risks. For example, business processes and activity spans must be such that economies of scope are achieved. This means that for example, you are not getting enough e-waste, can you include other metal scrap as a part of your activity? This will expand the scope of your business. For example, can you think about furniture refurbishing as an aligned activity? This would ensure maximum protection in case one of the activity suffers from an external problem. Professional business process consultants can integrate such processes within the main business.

Apart from these, there may be certain other risks, some of which you may have listed in the threats section of your SWOT analysis.

Risk of inability to meet target collections: This is a business failure risk. The total quantity of e-waste in India was projected to touch 1600,000 Tons by 2017 (ToxicsLink, MoEF, MPCB). In reality, this mark has been crossed in 2015. As of the beginning of 2020, unverified sources say that the e-waste generation of India has crossed 2 million tons. Of this, the total installed capacity of the organized e-waste recycling sector in India is currently at around 200,000 Tons. The unorganized sector accounts for a much larger fraction. No official data on the same is available. A generally accepted number is at around 300-400,000 tons. However, this is a fragmented capacity spread all over and no single facility may be more than 50-100 tons (Data from the unorganized sector, obtained through individual sources.) Therefore with a right level of effort in terms of a reverse logistics network and effective marketing the situation of not meeting collection targets should not arise.

This risk is essentially the same as the risk of not meeting sales targets for any company. So the same techniques of aggressive marketing, promotions and affiliate networks will solve this problem.

Risk of a slump in metal markets: Metals are clearly in limited quantities on the earth's surface. The demand for metals for various reasons is also clearly rising year on year. Both these facts put together, the demand-supply relation is increasingly skewing. Therefore, an isolated phenomenon of a metal market slump is almost impossible. However, a global recession may not be ruled out. In that case, along with metal markets, all other markets may also fall and the losses from the metal markets may be compensated through reduced expenses. (Scrap markets, labour markets, etc). Also, metals being a common trading commodity, they are also subject to speculative pressures. But speculative fluctuations are temporary in nature and they work both ways. So as a businessman you can use your acumen to understand market sentiment and offload or hold inventory to take advantage of these challenges.

Risk of Technology change: It is common knowledge that technology is changing at a fast pace. This may lead to a change in the composition of ICT equipment and thereby affect projected revenues. However, if we examine the technology advancements of the past we can clearly see the following trends :

a. Miniaturization. : Example – PCs to Laptops. In this case, the impact on a recycling business is that the collection targets are met by collecting more units. These additional units are made possible by more availability due to more widespread usage. With a reduction in sizes and costs, and aided by the generally growing affluence of Indian population, expansion of organizations etc, the ICT usage penetration is growing at a pace faster than the technology change. As a result, we see that more tonnage of ICT goods are shipped in India year on year. Therefore, this perceived risk is, in reality, a blessing to the resposal business. Also, the resale market for such products is very high and immensely profitable.

b. Demand for increased performance: Due to demand for increased performance and reduced sizes, higher power efficiencies etc, the precious metal content in ICT goods is actually going up in terms of percentage. The composition is also changing. In many components, gold is being replaced by silver. Silver being highly corrosive in nature, the life of such equipment goes down, boosting the rate of generation of scrap. However as of now, the electrical properties of gold remain unchallenged and where high-end technology and high performances are expected, the percentage of gold is on the rise. Therefore while this risk remains a very valid risk, little can be said conclusively about it. It may actually not matter much from a recycler's perspective.

c. A decrease in inefficient technologies (example: CRTs, power supplies): All technology advancement has an unmistakable characteristic of increasing efficiency. CRT replacement by TFT has ensured that space and energy are used more efficiently. However, the electronic circuitry required for TFTs is more complex than that required for CRTs. Therefore, the precious metal content of TFT is almost the same as CRT (minus the copper and aluminium).

Risk of cost escalation due to the unrecyclable waste residue after processing: Of all scrap collected, we have assumed that 20% is active components and 80 % is passive components. Of 80% passive components (example: Cabinets), the recycling rate is ~100%. Everything that goes in passive components (except the paint) is recyclable. Of the 20% active components, we are able to extract about 50%. Therefore the residue is only about 10%. Of this 10%, a major component is the PCB surface which is mostly epoxy. Fine powder of PCB surface boards is a very effective filler agent in the construction industry. Especially for roads, pavement blocks, prefabricated concrete items, there is a large demand for this powder. The actual 'waste' that needs to be discarded is only about 3-4% of the weight of the entire collection. Thus at full capacity, the hazardous disposal is only about 30-40 tons in an entire year. Pollution control boards allow hazardous material disposal at a fee. The cost of disposal of this fraction may be easily absorbed in miscellaneous expenses.

Increase in the competition is yet another risk. However as pointed out earlier, this risk is insignificant because the market potential is so high that there is enough room for many more players. Plus in an expanding market, competition doesn't really matter.

These and some other unforeseen risks may exist. But that is true for any business. There is nothing like a risk-free profitable business.

Action time

You have already listed down some threats in your SWOT analysis. Try to expand this list. These threats are your risks. Think about which of your strength can be used to overcome this risk. Think about which of the opportunities that you foresee have the potential of being a natural mitigation for the threats. You can summarize your finding in a simple tabular format.

Chapter 11

Regulations and compliances

Let me warn you about a very boring reading in this chapter. I would suggest to read it anyway because ignorance of the law is a crime. Especially when you are getting in a business, you must be aware of all the rules, regulations and compliances that are relevant to your business. For an e-waste business, we need to know international as well as national regulations.

International Regulations

The Basel Convention: "The Basel Convention on the Control of Transboundary Movements of Hazardous Wastes and their Disposal" is a global agreement that establishes the international legal regime governing the transboundary movement of hazardous wastes for disposal or recycling. Currently, 169 countries and the European Community have become Parties to the Convention. Parties meet their obligations through domestic regulations that implement the Convention. Interestingly the USA, the largest generator of e-waste has agreed to, but not ratified the Basel Convention yet. This means that the USA is not bound to operate by the conditions of the convention. Therefore, the USA continues to export its e-waste to buyers in other countries.

Transboundary movements: The Basel Convention imposes prior notification and consent controls on cross-border shipments of covered hazardous wastes between Parties. Transboundary movements of hazardous wastes between Parties and non-Parties in the absence of an appropriate "Article 11" agreement are prohibited. (Article 11 Agreement governs hazardous waste classifications and notice and consent procedures for shipments of waste for recycling)

Governments are obligated to ensure that waste shipments are only processed where the wastes can be managed in an "environmentally sound manner" in the countries of import. Waste trafficking is penalized and sanctions vary according to each party's legislation.

Basel Convention definition of e-waste: End-of-use electronic equipment that meets the Basel Convention's definitions for "waste" and "hazardous waste" is covered under import and export controls and shipment prohibitions under the Convention.

The Basel Convention defines wastes broadly as substances or objects which are disposed of or are intended to be disposed of or are required to be disposed of by the provisions of national law. The Convention then defines disposal by reference to lists of disposal operations, such as landfill or incineration, including recycling operations. Repair of computer equipment, however, is not a listed operation, and so computer equipment that is truly intended to be repaired is not defined as waste.

Basel Convention hazardous wastes: Equipment classified as waste that is derived from waste streams or contains a constituent listed in Annex I of the Convention (e.g. lead, cadmium, mercury, beryllium) is presumed to be hazardous unless it can be demonstrated that the waste does not possess any hazardous characteristics provided under Annex III. The Basel Convention does not provide any guidance on the development of testing protocols, leaving their design and implementation to national governments. However, for specific waste streams, technical guidelines have been adopted for implementation by Parties. The Convention provides further classification guidance on the classification of electronic equipment.

Other regulations: The European directive 2002/196/EC related to the WEEE

(Waste Electronic and Electrical Equipment) published in January 2003 defines the concept of Extended Producer Responsibility (EPR) concerning the collection of WEEE, the systematic treatment of hazardous parts, the recovery of all the WEEE collected, with priority given to reuse and recycling, and also to eco-design. In countries with EPR laws like the EU, some US states and Japan, electronics manufacturers are financially responsible for dealing with the waste from their products, meeting collection and recycling targets and other obligations. However, EPR only applies to domestically generated wastes. Some countries have also started to establish their own policies in order to ensure the quality of inbound shipments of used e-equipment. An entrepreneur in the business of repairing used computer equipment should be sure that the laws of his country, and of any country from which the used computer equipment has been imported, have been followed.

Indian Regulations

In India, e-waste trade comes under the broad regulatory framework related to the environment, foreign trade and local rules & regulations. Electronic waste is covered under hazardous waste in India. The Environment (Protection) Act 1986, an umbrella act covers hazardous waste and provides broad guidelines to address it.

India is a signatory to Basel Convention on the control of the trans-boundary movement of Hazardous Wastes and Disposal. The ratification of this convention obliges India to address the problem of transboundary movement and disposal of dangerous hazardous wastes through international cooperation.

The Ministry of Environment and Forests (MoEF) has issued the following notifications related to hazardous wastes:

1. Hazardous Wastes (Management and Handling) Rules, 1989/2000/2002
2. MoEF Guidelines for Management and Handling of Hazardous Wastes,1991
3. Guidelines for Safe Road Transport of Hazardous Chemicals,1995
4. The Public Liability Act, 1991
5. Batteries (Management and Handling) Rules, 2001
6. The National Environmental Tribunal Act, 1995
7. Bio-Medical Wastes (Management and Handling) Rules, 1998

8. Municipal Solid Wastes (Management and Handling) Rules, 2000 and 2002
9. MOEF e-Waste recycling rules and notification, 2015
10. MOEF Guidelines for e-waste management, 2016

The schedule listing 18 categories of wastes in the Hazardous Wastes (Management & Handling) Rules, 1989 has now been replaced by 3 schedules.

Schedule 1: Describes the processes and waste streams generating hazardous waste. Units operating these processes are now subject to the rules.

Schedule 2: Lists the concentration limits of constituents in the wastes. This concentration limit is to be used for classification/characterization of the waste stream as hazardous/non-hazardous in case of a dispute.

Schedule 3: Provides a separate list of wastes subject to export and import, similar to the Basel Convention Annexes VIII and IX

Responsibility for the identification of sites for the establishment of Common Treatment, Storage and Disposal Facilities (CTSDF) and individual TSDF now rests with the occupier, industrial association and the State Government alone.

Provisions relating to the import and export of hazardous waste for recycling have been expanded to describe in detail the procedure being followed. Requirements of the re-export of illegal traffic of waste under the Basel Convention have also been incorporated.

A manifest system has been introduced for tracking hazardous waste from the point of generation to the disposal site.

Authorities responsible for the regulation of imports and exports and monitoring the implementation of provisions of the rules have been mentioned in schedule 4, and a fee for authorization and import has been prescribed

Besides these rules, the Ministry of Environment and Forests (MoEF), New Delhi has issued guidelines for management and handling of hazardous wastes for (a) generators of waste, (b) transport of hazardous waste, and (c) owners/operators of hazardous waste storage, treatment and disposal facilities. These guidelines also establish mechanisms for the development of a reporting system for the movement of hazardous waste (the manifest system) and procedures for closure and post-closure requirements for landfills.

In addition to these direct rules dealing with issues of hazardous waste management, the Government has moved to enact legislation and additional incentives for industries to comply with environmental provisions and bring out market forces into the business of the environment. The Public Liability Act 1991, requires industries dealing with hazards to insure against accidents or damages caused by the release of pollutants.

Batteries (Management and Handling) Rules, 2001 apply to every manufacturer, importer, re-conditioner, assembler, dealer, recycler, auctioneer, consumer and bulk consumer involved in manufacture, processing, sale, purchase and use of batteries or components thereof. These rules confer responsibilities on the manufacturer, importer, assembler and re-conditioner; they govern the registration of importers, the customs clearance of imports of new lead-acid batteries, procedures for registration/ renewal of registration of recyclers and also the responsibilities of consumer or bulk consumer and responsibilities of auctioneers.

Guidelines for Safe Road Transport of Hazardous Chemicals (1995) establish basic rules for Hazardous Goods Transport and provided for the establishment of a Transport Emergency Plan and for provisions on Identification and assessment of Hazards.

The National Environmental Tribunal Act, 1995, provides for expeditious remedies to parties injured by environmental crimes. Legislation on the Community's Right to Know, 1996, has been adopted to provide more access to information regarding potential hazards from industrial operations.

Several enforcement agencies assist the Ministry of Environment and Forests at the state level in executing the assigned responsibilities. The Central Pollution Control Board advises on the policy and enforcement. State pollution control boards carry out enforcement at the state level.

Hazardous Waste Management Rules – Export & Import Issues

As per Basel Convention, India cannot export hazardous wastes listed in Annex VIII of the convention from the countries that have ratified the ban agreement. However, the convention agreement does not restrict the import of such wastes from countries that have not ratified the Basel Convention. It is through the orders of the Hon. Supreme Court of India that the import of such wastes is now banned in the country.

The HW Rules of 1989 control the import of hazardous wastes from any part of the world into India. Under the HWM Rules of 1989, the MoEF and the SPCB are the two recognised statutory organizations to ensure effective approval of import of hazardous wastes in the country. Under the new amendment of HWM Rules of 2002, List A and B of the Basel convention were introduced as Schedule 3 of the HWM Rules including the provisions relating to illegal traffic.

As per Rule 11 of HW Rules of 1989, import of wastes from any country to India shall not be permitted for dumping and disposal. However, import of such wastes may be allowed for processing or reuse as raw material, after each case has been examined on merit by the State Pollution Control Board. The SPCBs will examine applications from importers and forward such applications with its recommendations and requisite stipulations for safe transport, storage and processing/ disposal to the MoEF.

The Rules also require that hazardous wastes be packed and labelled during transport and that they will be deposited in waste disposal sites selected by the state government after an environmental impact assessment study.

Any importer wishing to import hazardous wastes must fill in the necessary information in Form 6 along with a fee of Rs. 30,000 for imports of up to 500 tonnes (extra Rs. 5000 for every additional 500 tonnes) to the SPCB/CPCB 125 days in advance.

As per the HW Rules, 1989/2000/2002, permissions to importers/exporters will be granted by the MoEF only, under Rules 13 (3) and 14 (3). Under this rule, the MoEF must satisfy itself that the importer has environmentally friendly/appropriate technology for reprocessing; that the importer has the capability to handle and reprocess hazardous wastes in an environmentally sound manner; and that the importer has adequate facilities for treatment and disposal of wastes generated.

Under Rule 14 (3), the MoEF must also consider and approve applications sent by exporters of consignments of hazardous wastes to India (Rule 11 of the un-amended HW Rules, 1989).

Current Legal System and E-Waste Trade:

As per India's export-import policy, new electronic goods can be freely imported in India. However, for old and junk electronics, there are complexities in the statutory provisions for the import because of confusions with provisions for the import of old computers in the Customs Tariff Act. Though there is a clear reference to the import of new computers in the Act, a similar provision does not exist for old computers.

However, the Indian government has a policy to promote the import of old computers. As per the recommendation of the National Task Force on Information Technology and Software Development, the Government of India in its 2001-02 budget has made a clear stipulation for the import of old computers as donations. As per the recommendation, the tax incentives for donations to institutions such as educational ones and hospitals have been increased. The incentives include the zero custom duty, exemption from gift and income taxes for both donors and receivers of PCs up to Rs.50, 000/-.

Under the Foreign Trade (Development and Regulation) Act of 1992, the Central Government has also provided for donations of computers and peripherals from zones which have been set up primarily for export - EOU (Export Oriented Units), EPZ (Exports Processing Zones), STP (Software Technology Parks) and EHTP (Electronics Hardware Technology Parks)-at a zero custom duty (Customs Notification No.47/98 dated 16 July 1998). Units in EOU/EPZ/STP/EHTP can donate computers and peripherals after two years of import and use, to recognized non-commercial educational institutions, registered charitable hospitals, public libraries, public-funded research &development establishments, organizations of the Government of India, or Government of State or Union Territory.

Though import of old PCs for the above-mentioned purposes is duty-free, it does not take place through the 'free' list. Import of old PCs requires a special license, under an 'actual user condition'. The 'actual user condition' clause of the Foreign Trade (Development and Regulation) Act 1992 debars resale for reuse or recycling. It stipulates: "In case of imports under license/ certification/ permission, the actual user alone may import such goods unless the actual user condition is specifically dispensed with by the licensing authority". Till date, Directorate General of Foreign Trade (DGFT) has not dispensed such conditionality in any instance.

Finally, under the International Basel Convention on the Trans-boundary Movement of Hazardous Wastes, to which India is a signatory, the Ministry of Environment and Forests has to give a prior permission to any hazardous imports. This is as per the provisions of the Hazardous Waste Management and Handling Rules 1989 as amended in 2000 (under the Environment Protection Act,1986), in Schedule −3, List A and List B. Computer waste falls under such categories, and according to the Ministry, no such permission has been granted to date.

However, thanks to the loopholes in the present legal system, such trade in WEEE for recycling and resale is taking place. As per Indian laws, computers more than 10-year-old come under the category of junk computers and the Indian custom law does not recognize their trade. However, a 9-year-old PC is not classified as junk. In fact, the term "junk computer" does not exist in the internationally accepted Harmonized Tariff System. However, the possibility of such detection is minimal because the checking of each container is almost impossible. The Directorate General of Foreign Trade is the prime certifying authority in case of imports of second-hand goods.

Drawbacks of the Current Legal System

Flexible interpretations of the rules framed by the DGFT. In order to check and detect the illegal import of old PCs (import without a license), Customs Authorities have been delegated power to make on-the-spot decisions, going from the confiscation of goods to the imposition of fines on such imports. However, after the imposition of a fine, importers are allowed to take possession of the goods. Under-assessment of illegally imported goods is also common.

There is no Exim code for trade in second-hand computers for donation purpose or for resale. Both second-hand and new computers are classified under chapter 84 of the Indian Customs Tariff Act. Thus, trade data for new computers includes data for old computers. Taking advantage of this, exporters sometimes club old and junk computers along with new ones.

Taking advantage of the flexibility in the interpretation of rules, some Port Authorities also make a distinction between capital goods and non-capital goods in order to facilitate the import of told PCs. For them, old computers imported as a donation to educational or charitable institutions come under the 'capital goods' category. As capital goods, they are then under the free list and access various tax benefits.

Other old computers (less than 10-year old) imported for the purpose of resale or recycling come under the 'non-capital goods' category and can only be imported against a license. In order to avoid the burden of high taxes, in case of import under non-capital goods category, importers may under-invoice goods. The liberal position taken by the Customs Authority for keeping imported old PCs under capital goods in the free list directly conflicts the position taken by the representatives of DGFT.

Several integrated HTPFs, EOUs, EPZs, etc. have been set up by the Government of India to meet specific requirements of a globally oriented electronics hardware sector. 100%Export Oriented Units can also be established outside these zones, anywhere in India, and all the incentives available to EPZs units and so on are also available to the EOUs.

Electronic Waste and Environmental Legislation in India

Despite a wide range of environmental legislation in India, there are no specific laws or guidelines for electronic waste or computer waste. The current e-waste handling rules have come into effect from April 2012 and undergone a few amendments in 2016 and 2018.

Extended Producer Responsibility.

The latest development in the Indian scenario is the gazetted e-waste handling and management rules. This includes the crucial provision for enforcing extended producer responsibility as a law. Under this provision, all manufacturers of electrical and electronic goods have a mandatory responsibility of ensuring that all the waste that is generated in their manufacturing processes as well as due to end of life products is collected and provided for recycling. The manufacturers are responsible to set up the required financial and logistical structure for the same. Manufacturers are free to establish such a mechanism either on their own or through a contractual relationship with certified agencies commonly called PRO.

You can study more of these regulations from the website of the Ministry of Environment and Forests, Government of India.

The process to start an e-waste recycling facility

e-Waste recycling is a controlled industry in India due to its high pollution potential. You need to be registered as an authorised recycling unit with the state pollution control board. The process is as under :

Step 1: Apply for "consent to establish"

This step is an essential starting point. You need to submit a business plan, technology, business process and a statement of environmental impact along with the application form. Apart from that, the financial viability is also required. The list of documents that need to be submitted also include a NOC from the local body, an industry registration such as SSI or MSME or SME or any other, details of the land on which the project is proposed to be commissioned, a letter from the local electricity board and water supply department stating their in-principle agreement to supply the required power and water respectively for the project, etc.

Step 2: Apply for registration

Once the Consent to Establish is granted, you can start the process of commissioning of the project. At this stage, you can also simultaneously apply for registration of the unit. This application form contains almost similar details as in the CoE. However this time, they are in a little more detail. As a part of the registration process, you may need to deliver a presentation in front of an expert panel explaining the process, the operation of the machinery and the environmental amelioration provisions included.

Step 3: Apply for "consent to operate"

At this stage, officials from the pollution control board may visit your facility and inspect a test run. Based on their inspection, and subject to their satisfaction about the anti-pollution measures, they can grant a consent to operate.

This entire process of application is completely online. Each state pollution control board has an online application portal. You can legally start commercial activities only after the last stage i.e the consent to operate.

Compliances

Apart from regulatory restrictions, worldwide there are certain compliances and standards established for the e-waste industry to follow. Europe follows the e-stewards standard. This is very stringent compliance and the focus is on pollution control in the entire recycling process. This is one of the strictest standards.

R2 certification is another standard. This is promoted by an organization called SERI. This US-based standard is a little more lenient than e-stewards but equally effective. The good part about R2 is that it also takes into consideration processes used for refurbishing and software license related compliances.

OHSAS 18001 and ISO 14000 are the basic environmental standards that every e-waste recycler should ideally comply with. While the pollution control board does not require you to comply with these standards, it is a useful badge to have when you are competing in the markets. Also, these are fundamental requirements before you can apply for R2 or e-Stewards.

You can simply engage a standards auditor for getting these certifications. This lead auditor will help you with all the paperwork and the process-related aspects of compliances. Ideally, when the shopfloor processes are designed they should be designed with these compliances in mind so that getting these certifications becomes very easy.

Action Time

List down all the certifications that you will need.

List down key regulations that you need to follow.

Ensure that these are a part of your key considerations.

Chapter 12

Putting it all together – business plan

In business, it is good to have your project plan A and an emergency plan B. You are likely to discover that usually a plan C will succeed! And more often than not, plan C gets written as you go along with your business. But if this is the case what good does it serve to write a project plan A in the first place? Well, you understand a lot of things beforehand. You get a hang of what could be in store and unwanted surprises are minimized.

Besides, your banker will ask you for a project plan. You will need a project plan to entice your team members. You will need your project plan to even know what to do next. Chances are good that you will keep rewriting the plan as you go along. However, my advice is that it is good to rewrite the business plan from the thick of the battlefield. No amount of closed-door strategy will help you ever. It is only good to inspire you and give you a morale boost. Rest will need to be action-based.

Despite this, you still need a business plan. Writing a business plan is not an easy task. A ready-made generic project report is not good either. If you want to outsource this project report writing you should at least make sure that it is not generic and written specifically for your company.

However, you may not get anyone with these skills easily. The good news is that after having read this book and gone through all the exercises at the end of each chapter, you are well equipped to write an impressive business plan.

So let us recap the learnings from all the previous 11 chapters. You can simply compile all the exercises from each of these chapters and it serves as a baseline for your project report or business plan document. Now you just need to put things in a nice looking format.

Your business plan document should ideally use the following template.

Executive summary

This should be a quick overview saying what the project is about, why it is needed, the total investment and the profitability/viability. About a page is good enough. If you are making the business plan as a presentation, you can use a single slide.

Introduction

A good introduction will talk about you, your company, why you intend to get into this business and how you intend to do it. Two to three pages or a single presentation slide should suffice.

Market overview

This book has given you good insights into various aspects of the market. You can do your own surveys and studies and add to the information provided in this book to write this market overview. Ideally, it should have the total market size, your addressable market, how you intend to address the same, who your competition is likely to be and what are the essential characteristics and behavioural traits of your potential customers.

Operations overview

This section should summarize the business process that you would follow and the technologies that will be used in your facility. A clear flowchart will be helpful. You may use the flowcharts and the factory layouts shown in this book or you may use your own modifications of the same. This section must also give a clarity about the environmental aspects of your operations, the emissions or effluents at each stage and how you intend to control the pollution arising at every stage of operations. This is of key concern to the pollution control board while giving you the consent to establish.

Financial analysis

This section is most important for the financers. You can give just the final projected financial performance sheets or arrive at them through a logical method used in this book. Either way, you will need to keep a backup of your workings because the financer will ask you a lot of questions and you will need to justify every number that you have put there.

You can use the following template for the financial statements. If you wish, you may modify the same to suit your convenience.

Projected profit and loss statement

	Year 1	Year 2	Year 3
Revenue from Sales			
Operating Expenses			
Salaries			
Rent			
Raw Material			
Utilities			
Transportation			
Spares and consumables			
Directors Compensation			
Others and Contingency			
Total			
PBIDT			
Interest Paid			
Depreciation (on p&m @ 15 %, WDV)			
Depreciation (on building @ 5 %, WDV)			
PBT			
Tax @ 25%			
PAT			

Dividend paid			
Tax on dividend @ 17%			
Transferred to General Reserves			

Projected cash flow statement

	Year 1	Year 2	Year 3
Cash Receipts			
Opening Cash Balance			
Share Capital			
Bank loan			
PBIDT			
Total			
Cash Payments			
Capex (for plant and machinery)			
Capex (for Building)			
Repayment of principal			
Interest on loans			
Depreciation on machinery (10 yrs, WDV)			
Depreciation (on building @ 5 %, WDV)			
Taxes @ 25%			
Dividend			
Tax on dividend@17%			
Total			
Closing Cash Balance			

Projected balance sheet

	Year 1	Year 2	Year 3
Sources of Funds			
Owner's equity			
Share Capital			
Reserves and Surplus			
Loan Funds			
Secured loan			
Total			
Application of Funds			
Fixed assets			
Plant and Machinery			
Less Accumulated Depreciation			
Building			
Less Accumulated Depreciation			
Net Block			
Current Assets			
Cash (Working Capital + WIP Inventory)			
Less Current Liabilities			
Total Current Liabilities			
Net Current Assets			
Total Assets			

Risk analysis

You can start this section with your SWOT analysis. Further, you can mention the risks and use the SWOT analysis to explain how you intend to mitigate these risks.

Annexures: You may decide to add certain annexures including proposals from your vendors, your own accreditations etc.

Ideally, you should have the business plan both as a text document and as a presentation. Depending on your audience, you can use the correct format. Ideally, for government purposes, use the text format. For financers, it is ideal that you deliver the presentation in person and then hand over the printed slides and a printout or a softcopy of your financial calculations. Remember that your investor also sees and reads many things other than the written word. Use it for your benefit. Your passion and conviction must be communicated through your presentation. A passive text document cannot convey that. This will help in building trust with your investor.

Also, your investor may ask you about your plan B. You may well have it in your back pocket. But don't rush to share it with him. Typically a plan B will be similar with a reduced scope and scale at the beginning and a rapid ramp-up in later years. In our plan A, we have assumed a constant rise of 20% year on year. In plan B it could be starting at a smaller capacity and the rate of growth may start at 10%

and the rate of growth itself may accelerate 25% year on year.

Finally, even if after everything, if you don't get funded, don't lose heart. Knock the next door. Or you may choose the easier option to start small with business model 1 of dismantling only and that too at a lower scale. Simultaneously you can keep looking for funding. In fact, your chances of getting funded are higher if you are already in the business.

And finally, the gem of advice, if it is your own money and your own business plan, treat yourself like an investor and the guy in the mirror as the startup entrepreneur. Be hard on yourself. It is your hard-earned money. You cant throw it away behind a crazy idea even if it is your own!

Once you have done this kind of due diligence and you get in the business, not for the promise of the money, but for the value that you promise to create, you can make a difference. I may be repeating the same thing, but trust me, it is your passion that will eventually work. The money will come. But your passion will fuel your business. It is you who would make the difference. This could be your chance to create a lasting impact, recycle e-waste, and grow rich!

Action Time

Go ahead. Write your business plan. Convert that into a presentation format. Show it to friends. Hear out their suggestions. Keep a critic by your side. Your strongest critic is your best friend. Once done, show the plan to a couple of investors. Most likely, you will get turned down by most of them. With every rejection, make sure you ask them their reasons for rejection. Use that information to strengthen your plan. Finally, one last word, do not wait for funding. Get going with whatever small scale you can. It will help to serve as a proof of your business plan. It will also help to refine your business plan with first had wisdom. And ultimately, it is always easy to get funding for a proven and running business!

About the Author

D.B. Prabhu alias Nahoosh was born in 1972 in Dombivli - a then-obscure distant suburb of Mumbai. He spent his childhood in rural areas of western India where he learned at all places other than at school. At the age of 5, he ran away from his vernacular school to study English, a fascination for which he derived from his doctor neighbour. Three years later Nahoosh was penning his first creative expressions in his mother tongue, the same Marathi language that he had escaped from.

He switched on to his official name - Dwarkanath Prabhu - at the age of ten when he moved back to Mumbai from where he completed his schooling. Prabhu later completed his graduation in engineering, Executive MBA and a full-time Masters degree - Post-Graduation in public policy and management from IIM Bangalore, arguably one of the best management schools in Asia. During his IIM days, he worked extensively in the field of technological interventions for social change, education, poverty alleviation, and environmental amelioration and published a few papers in peer-reviewed academic journals on the subjects.

Prabhu's career started and flourished in the information technology industry where he worked as a business - technology optimization consultant for more than two decades. He further expanded his horizons by co-founding Respose Waste Management and Research Pvt Ltd, a company dedicated to creating profitable green entrepreneurial ventures.

Currently, besides being a business mentor for startups, especially in the technology and environmental space, Prabhu writes fiction, creative non-fiction and business and entrepreneurial books.

He has to his credit two books – a romance fiction - Love, Karma, Destiny and a poetic memoir – Musings published under his alias Nahoosh.

Coming Up Soon

Mining Green Gold – 25 ideas in environment centric businesses

By

DB Prabhu

Founder and CEO of

Respose Waste Management and Research Pvt. Ltd.

It is a general misconception that environment centric activities are charity based and need to be funded by the government or large corporate houses. However, the environment provides limitless opportunities. A bit of different thinking can help in creating interesting businesses based around the environmental cause.

All of these businesses can be profitable, scalable and replicable. This book summarizes 25 such ideas and gives a clear roadmap for a complete overhaul in the way we have created our economic order.

To avail of a prelaunch discount, you can book your copy on the website https://www.resposeindia.com/books. More details about this book are available on the above weblink.